What's the Story? Storytelling with Young Children as a Path Toward Living Happily Ever After

by
Stephen Spitalny

What's the Story: Storytelling with Young Children as a Path
     Toward Happily Ever After

©2015 by Stephen Spitalny

First Printing 2015

ISBN 978-1-329-15168-0

Chamakanda Press
www.chamakanda.com

What's the Story? Storytelling with Young Children as a Path Toward Living Happily Ever After

by
Stephen Spitalny

Contents

Introduction

The best of the stories we can give our children, whether they are stories that have been kept alive through the centuries through that mouth-to-mouth resuscitation we call oral transmission, or the tales that were made up only yesterday - the best of these stories touch that larger dream, that greater vision, that infinite unknowing. They are the most potent kind of magic, these tales, for they catch a glimpse of the soul beneath the skin.
Touch magic. Pass it on.
Jane Yolen

I love stories. I love to read stories and listen to stories. I love to tell stories. I love creating stories. Stories are enriching and nourishing. In a story I can experience other people, other cultures, other worlds - all that is other - and that gives me perspective on my own situation. Stories inform my reality, perspectives and experiences and help to give me context.

I love books. My own library includes many books of folk and fairy tales from around the world. I have a large collection of "picture books," even including some from my own childhood. When I go to book stores and libraries, I always check the "children's" book section and the folk and fairy tale section for anything new (or old) that I might be interested in. And I have a repertoire of twenty or thirty stories that I can tell by heart on the spur of the moment.

I think stories are an essential part of early childhood. The world of stories is rich with images that can help guide a young child along their path of growing into this life on planet earth. Stories help shape the young listener and can support the development of various characteristics and qualities that will serve the individual throughout life.

This book includes ideas about many aspects of stories, and ideas about how to make stories in general and stories specifically to help change behaviors in your young children. My intention is to keep it short and simple so you, the reader, can enter and be comfortable in the fantastic world of story. The gift of a world of story can enrich your life and the lives of those around you, especially the young children. Story allows us, young and old, to make sense of the world around us and to have hope for getting through challenges towards a better world.

Chapter 1
What is a story?

At its most basic, a story depicts a sequence of events. It has a beginning, a middle and an end. A story describes a situation that unfolds over time. A story can be a teaching, a symbol, and a distilling of something that is much larger and all encompassing. Through story we can find meaning in our lives. Story is a mechanism by which we process and attribute meaning to our world. Young and old alike, we are irresistibly attracted to stories. We have a hunger for the images we can find in stories.

The first stories were probably sequences of pictures describing food opportunities and dangers to be avoided. They were survival related. The content of the earliest human speech was likely also related to these survival needs. Our ancient ancestors expressed in story their fears and their explanations about how the world worked. It seems it is a basic human need to put our experiences into a narrative form.

The theory I'm putting forward here is that storytelling is a genetic characteristic in the sense that early human hunters who were able to organize events into stories were more successful than hunters who weren't—and this success translated directly into reproductive success. In other words, hunters who were storytellers tended to be better represented in the gene pool than hunters who weren't, which (incidentally) accounts for the fact that storytelling isn't just found here and there among human cultures, it's found universally. Daniel Quinn (*The Story of B: An Adventure of the Mind and Spirit*)

There is a hunger in us for story, for the flow of images that describes the metamorphosis of situations. Our modern culture is full of stories; traditional stories, written stories, published books, movies, and more. The advertising industry and our governments rely on our hunger for story and they try to write our story for us. 'This is what you need to be able to accomplish your goals.' The goals also are instilled by advertisers, but that is another story. The news media tries to give us the story of what is going on and what led up to it, always with the spin of the journalists' particular perspectives. We end up with an unhealthy craving instead of a simple hunger.

The sage Vyasa, author of the 'Mahabarata'...said that if we listen carefully to a story we will never be the same again. The story, especially if it has some spiritual basis, will worm its way into our heart and break down our self-constructed barriers to the divine. Even if we start off by reading these stories as entertainment, one or two of them will eventually slip through our defenses and explode the hard shell of our humanity to disclose our divinity. Vanamali (*Hanuman: The Devotion and Power of the Monkey God*)

Our soul is hungry for the information we receive from the flow of images in stories, and we are continually asking ourselves, 'Are these images true? Is this true for me?' That is how we exercise the thinking of the heart. In our time of the exalted god of analytical, intellectual thinking, the thinking of the heart is undervalued and under-used. We are being fed a bill of goods that says that the human being is a computer. That is surely not the whole story. The creative side of the brain, the non-computer aspects, is home to imagination. The heart determines if imaginations are true. Through listening to and digesting stories, our heart and brain can learn to work together and we can become more fully integrated human beings.

Arguing with someone is a clash of ideas and opinions and uutilizes the intellect. To truly change someone's mind, we have to reach their his or her heart. Story is a tool for this. Many great teachers over the millennia have used stories as teaching tools. The magical power of story lies in the fact that it is received by the heart, not the head. Stories that the heart feels are true become part of one's reality, part of one's structure, even all the way down into the physical body. Seriously. This is powerful stuff. It can be medicine!

> *I have learned that the head does not hear anything*
> *until the heart has listened, and what the heart knows*
> *today the head will understand tomorrow.*
> James Stephens

When we allow a story in, we bypass the intellect. After a story, we say; "I loved that story," or "I didn't like that one." We don't respond to a story with, "I disagree with that," or "That's not correct." We respond with our feelings, and it seeps into our thoughts later.

Storytelling is a healing art that can draw out the innate wisdom within us. Stories make us more aware of ourselves as part of feeling, creating. laughing, crying, curious, courageous humanity. Together they have a cumulative effect, broadening our inner knowing, our compassion, and our sense of self. They can also help us to nourish the body's natural intelligence by speaking directly to and from the intricate weave of our bodies.
Nancy Mellon (*Body Eloquence*)

With the newborn, the speaking of the people around her washes over her like a rainbow soundscape, at first with no comprehension on the infant's part. The flow of language is really a flow of sound not conceived of as words with meanings. The newborn child is a long way from experiencing a consciousness of self. The young child is deeply listening to the world, to nature. She understands in a basic, direct and non-conceptual way.

Little by little, the meaning of words arises so that the sounds of speech take on inner content. Through storytelling we can nurture the child's love of language. In stories, the child hears new phrases, ways of speaking, new ways of saying something and she expands her vocabulary. She learns meanings by hearing the words in context, and then experiments with words and grammar and syntax based on imitating the spoken language of those around her.

An important faculty that develops out of listening to stories is inner picturing. Being able to conjure up mental images, the inner representation of what the words signify, is an essential element of reading comprehension. Listening to stories is practice for this capacity.

Young children so easily learn stories by heart, even without comprehending the meaning. For the very young, stories are an opportunity for language to wash over them. They begin to taste the flavor of their mother tongue.

It is important to read and tell stories to young children that have happy endings where the difficulties are resolved and the tasks accomplished. The young child thrives when feeling that the world around them is a safe and just place where good prevails. Then the child relaxes into the path of their own becoming instead of being in a defensive and self-protective attitude.

Just as the child is born with a literal hole in its head, where the bones slowly close underneath the fragile shield of skin, so the child is born with a figurative hole in its heart. Slowly, this too is filled up. What slips in before it anneals, shapes the man or woman into which that child will grow.
Jane Yolen
(*Touch Magic: Fantasy, Faerie & Folklore in the Literature of Childhood*)

Chapter 2
What Does this Story Mean?

Stories are like living beings. Your relationship to a particular story develops and evolves over time. The story has new things to say to you and new comforts to offer. I always ask a story: "Who are you, and what are you trying to tell me now?"

I want to get to know the story and discover what it is saying to me. Some stories have become my old friends and treasured companions.

Thinking about symbolism and interpretation are activities of the intellect. The part of our brain where that sort of capacity resides is the prefrontal cortex which is very undeveloped in the young child and, in fact, is not fully mature until one is in their late twenties. Let the story speak for itself, don't do interpretation with the young children. Allow the young children their pre-intellectual dream-life where the imagination still reigns and the intellect has not yet risen to the throne.

I think this is important to grasp; the part of the brain that functions in reasoning, problem solving, comprehension, and impulse-control is the prefrontal cortex. These executive brain functions are needed when we have to focus and think, mentally play with ideas, use our short-term working memory, and think before reacting in any situation. Those functions are simply not yet available to the young child because the prefrontal cortex is in an early stage of its development.

The intellect of the young child is in its infancy. Extraneous information and explanation is unnecessary and can get in the way of receiving the story. While the cultural origins, symbolism and meaning of a story may be interesting to you with your developed intellect, for the child it is mental clutter.

The story itself speaks more strongly than any interpretation or moralizing can ever do.

My goal is to support young children in their process of gradual awakening, and not to awaken them into premature self consciousness and intellect. Before I tell a story, if I were to say; "This is the story of 'Brier Rose.' It is a Grimm's fairy tale from Germany and comes from 200 years ago," then I am distracting the child with abstract background information, even though it may be interesting to me. Presenting the story on its own is more conducive to the flow of the young child's life. In telling stories from Africa, Asia, Europe, North or South America, or wherever, describing the stories' origins and cultural backgrounds is unnecessary intellectual information. The children do not need that information. They do need the nourishment to their inner life that the stories provide. It is not yet the time to *teach* the children about the wide world, but a soul taste of stories from other cultures without abstract side notes supports their imaginative stage of development.

Later in this book, I offer my interpretations of some stories to give you an idea about how I process story images and attempt to connect to underlying meanings and guidance. Try not to be too attached to *my* thoughts about story symbolism.

Chapter 3
That Same Story Again and Again

As I mentioned before, I love books. I want children to grow up loving books too. If you want your children to become members of the world of readers, they need to see you reading, both to them and reading for your own pleasure and learning. Young children learn by imitating. That is the fundamental learning modality for the young child.

For me, books are an essential part of life and starting in early childhood there needs to be plenty of experience of books and reading. This can nurture the love of books that can last throughout life. Every bedtime deserves a story to help send the child off to dreamland. Everyday is the right day for a story.

You may have noticed your three- or four-year-old saying, immediately upon completion of a story, "Tell it again." Or when you sit down together for a storybook, she asks for the same one as yesterday. And again.....

"Oh no! How boring," you think to yourself. "Not that one again."

You have a developed intellect. Your intellect always wants more and different experiences. The young child has an undeveloped intellect and therefore cannot get bored. Instinctively she is asking for something supportive of her developing neurology. Repetition! Repetition supports developing neural pathways and the myelination process. Repetition supports developing neural pathways and the myelination process. So put aside your boredom and learn to enjoy the same story again. And again...

Chapter 4
The Gift of Telling Stories

All of the techniques of child rearing, helpful as they may be with respect to particular problems, cannot offer an adequate substitute for this necessary food of the child's soul. J. E. Heuscher, *(A Psychiatric Study of Myths and Fairy Tales)*

Sharing stories is a gateway to connection. Reading to a child is a wonderful shared experience. Telling a story without the book is a profound gift we can offer to our children, and to each other. A told story is given from the heart of the teller (we know a story by *heart*) to the heart of the listener. There is nothing like this gift and this activity is becoming rare. The oral tradition seems to be disappearing.

By telling a story to a child, rather than reading a story from a picture book, the child must create all of her own images, her own internal pictures, for the story. This inner activity is the basis for reading comprehension - the ability to create inner pictures from the words spoken.

This inner activity of attaching meaning to words and creating inner pictures supports the development of the prefrontal cortex because it is there that the conversion must be made from mere sound into verbal symbols and mental images.

Tell stories! Your young child is the most forgiving audience, and the most grateful. Give it a try.

Chapter 5
Tips on Storytelling Technique

When you tell a story or read a story to young children, try to see in your imagination what you say. Engage your own mental picturing capacity! For adults, it can be hard to use language not just as information but as active imagination, · as active flow of images. But that is what a story is.

A story is a series of images, a movement of pictures, not merely a set of words and phrases. When a storyteller inwardly "sees" the images of a story, the story becomes more alive for the children and other listeners. This is part of the art of storytelling, of the art of making stories come alive.

I like to simply offer the story to my young listeners, and get myself out of the way. What I mean is that I want what the child takes away to be the story itself, not my telling of the story. So I tell stories in a non-dramatic style. I don't have a monotonous telling style, but I am not trying to excite the feelings of the listener. The images themselves may do that, but as storyteller, I want to get out of the way so the story can speak. Rather than performance artist, I want to be like a channel for the delivery of the story. That way the child's own inner pictures are not determined by the teller's dramatic rendering style. I am not trying to stimulate the listeners' feelings, I am allowing the story to speak in its unique voice to each unique listener.

With young children, I like to tell the same story each day for as long as is possible. The younger the children, the longer the story can last. Even at kindergarten age, I can tell the same story everyday for weeks on end. When a story is repeated over days and weeks, it penetrates into the play of the children as well as into their developing neurology. Hence, an ideal is to repeat a story daily for as long as is possible.

If I am telling or reading an old tale, I respect the integrity of the story. I do not alter the plot, or water it down or romanticize it. I don't change the ending or soften the given consequences of actions. I leave that to the Disneys of the world. If I am not satisfied with the plot of a passed-down story as it is, I can find another story to tell. There are many!

It is important that a story is true for the person telling the story. A story told by a person who doesn't think it is truthful will fall on the deaf ears of the young child who sees right into us. Does this story resonate in your heart as true? If not, tell a different story.

When telling a story, consider your posture. Are you upright and relaxed? Are your arms or legs crossed? (Are you protecting yourself from the listeners?) If you are sitting in a chair, are you grounded with your feel flat on the floor? Is your posture saying that you believe what you are telling? Or does it say you are not so sure?

How do you decide if a story suits the prospective audience? First, are you as storyteller comfortable with the images, the pictures in the story? Does the story resonate with truth for you?

Then consider the audience in relation with the tasks in the particular story, and in relation with the meanness and evil present in the story.

Thinking about the particular young children I will be telling the story to and what they can digest:

How hard are the tasks?
How evil is evil?

There are no right answers for these. It is a matter for your own developed intuition. If you consider these questions, you *will* know.

Chapter 6
Storytelling as Medicine

Stories can be powerful tools for teaching, healing and transformation. When there is a behavior in your young child that you would like to see changed, an effective tool can be a story that portrays a similar situation and an outcome you'd like to see, an outcome different from the one you see the child in your life experiencing. You can rewrite the scenario with a changed behavior and a different unfolding of the story than you have experienced already with your child.

For example, if you notice your child is not as kind to animals as you would wish, consider telling her the story of *The Queen Bee* from the brothers Grimm. In this story, Simpleton, the youngest of three brothers, protects various creatures who later in the story return to help him accomplish difficult tasks. It is unnecessary to state the message; "You see. If you help the creatures they will help you." The story already so clearly and artfully delivers the message!

Stories are a wonderful vehicle to convey the values of the storyteller to the listener, the receiver of the story. With young children, it is an effective way to help change behaviors and create new habits without intellectualizing and explaining.

A story can help make a situation that is personal into one that is objective. This allows the listener to be open to a recasting of the script, a release of the old, personal story, and a rewriting of the response to the challenges. It can help to rewire the listener's neurology to allow for a different response and can help create new, more constructive habits.

You can support another individual, child or otherwise, by attempting a healing story for that other person. It can be about habits needing transforming, about awareness of others in a social setting, and it could even be on the level of physical healing. In a later section, I offer some tips and methods for creating just the right story for another person. You can even rewrite your own story as part of a personal healing journey.

As I mentioned earlier, it's normal for a child to want the same story over and over. As your young child get's older often they start wanting more variety. This is 'normal' too. Sometimes your slightly older young child latches onto a story and wants it again and again. They are not able to explain why that particular story speaks to them, and yet it does. Don't try to ask and ask questions, trying to mine the significance from your child's undeveloped intellect. Allow the story to be told. There might be some deep lesson your child intuits in the story. It might be helping your child to process something that neither you nor the child are aware of. Because the story does speak to your child, support that story as an important medicine for your child on some unknown level. Tell that story, read that story, as often as it is requested.

One of my daughters loved the Tomie dePaola book, *The Lady of Guadalupe.* She wanted me to read it over and over, day after day for many weeks. Why? I have no idea. The story is a lovely retelling of the appearance of the Lady of Guadalupe to a poor farmer in the 1500's, and the subsequent miracle of a painting appearing on his cloak. Did I read it to her when she wanted it over and over? I sure did. Did I ever discover what it was about that story that so appealed to her? No, it is still an open question.

Chapter 7
Our Own Story

We all have our own story. It is how we view ourselves in relation with the world. We rely on that personal story as our guide to interpreting our experiences. The amazing thing about human beings is that we can change our story to help ourselves overcome old patterns and habits that we no longer find useful.

Rewriting one's own story is not so easy to do. It is challenging to decide to rewrite, and commit to the new story. Yet we all have inside us an amazing, creative and powerful storyteller that is waiting to be allowed to speak.

A simple start is to think of your earliest experience in which your needs were not met. Perhaps you felt unsafe or wanting nurturing. I'm sure you can recall some such time in your past. Try to imagine what would have made that situation a better experience for you? Retell the story of the challenging situation as it could have been. Perhaps in your recasting of your story someone appears and gives you the help you needed. It could be that you yourself responded differently and created a different outcome. It could be that the other person in your story responded differently. Try different scenarios until you find one that feels right. And then tell your story to yourself over and over. Let it seep into you, wash over you, cleanse you and heal you.

This is no easy practice and is not to be taken lightly. Try it with 'smaller' challenging situations from your past before you attempt the big ones. Step by step approach your biggest challenges from your childhood, and rewrite them. It is as if you are rewriting yourself and making yourself into what you want, not a product of what happened to you. In this way we can take charge of our own past, become present and look forward to a better future.

A practice involving the writing of stories, the creating of your own stories, can be a tool for self-development. We also can learn how to help others transform and heal by the stories we create and tell to them, both adults and children. Wouldn't it be incredible if we could know just what story to tell a child, or a friend, to bring them the images they need to lessen their suffering and allow them to remove some of their own obstacles?

Chapter 8
Different Modes for Different Folks

The simplest way to tell a story is to open your mouth and let the words flow. Another mode for story is the puppet show. The puppet show is a way to make a story visible. Puppet shows can run the gamut from simple, small dolls on the ground or on your lap, to multi-stringed marionettes on a stage with scenery.

To allow the story to become fully a product of the child's own imagination, simple puppets work best. Elaborate puppets with defined faces and frozen gestures present an already finished image with no room for the child's imaginative participation.

If the child can see the stories unfold step-by-step, grow and change in the simple but beautiful way described, the pictures can be taken right into the stream of his life forces, without creating hard and fixed impressions...The simplicity and transparency of our [puppet] table plays calls forth the child's powers of imagination, and he is right in the midst of all that takes place. Through this, the creative power for his own play as well as for his own movement and language development are stimulated. In this way the child can also be helped to become a person of independence and creative activity in later life. Bronja Zahlingen

I like to use "table puppets," simple stuffed cloth dolls that can stand up without being held. I want the children to see my direct contact with the puppets as I take hold of them with my hands and move the puppets around on the table, the floor, or my lap. My example of simple puppets gives the children something that they are able to imitate, and they will end up doing their own puppet plays.

When making your puppets, there is the question of color. What colors does one use to represent what symbolic aspects of the story? What skin color to use to make the faces and bodies? This question becomes moot if the puppets have red or blue or purple faces as symbolic representation of the soul-spiritual qualities portrayed in the story.

Perhaps the old king and queen could be purple faced, clothed in gold. Simpleton could red with golden clothing. The North Wind can be blue and white cloths with a simple knot to hold on to. This way, the viewer, parent or child, can imagine what they choose and not experience the story as something that is not them.

Another mode for storytelling is acting out the story. This style is a developed art and is very challenging with the under five-year-olds. When I lead an 'acted out' story, I do the telling, and walk the children through the space in the room where I am telling so they can experience the movement of the story. Usually, unprompted, they will say the dialog along with me, though I don't ask or expect the young children to recite dialog lines.

One could even use simple capes, hats and crowns to add some color to the acted out story. The more elaborate the costuming, the more time is taken away from immersing in the story and the more chaos you might be allowing in. As with so many aspects of life with young children, simple is better!

Special note to teachers: There is a tradition in certain early childhood programs that the teacher first tells the story for one week. The next week it is presented as a puppet play, and then a third week is spent acting out the story at storytime.

I don't know where this tradition comes from and I don't agree with it. It doesn't resonate with my thinking. I think that when you tell a story, the listeners create their own inner pictures of the story - colors are included in that imagining. If you tell a story allowing those inner images to arise, and then present the same story as a puppet play with your imagining of color and costume, then you are likely creating a dissonance in the listener who may have different imagining of the colors in the same story.

My suggestion: If you are going to do a puppet play of a story, start on day one with that puppet play, and do it as a puppet play each day you do that story. If you tell the story first, skip the puppet play version. An acting out version of a story with very simple or no costumes and props still allows the listener's imagination to go wild in their own unique way.

Chapter 9
Remembering a Story by Heart

If you are going to repeat the same story many times to a child, it is important that you can tell it the same way every time. Then when you tell the story for the umpteenth time, the child can relax into their imaginative dreaminess. If they are used to a certain way of your telling, and then you change a word, it is a startling experience for the child. It shocks him out of that dreamy place into wakefulness.

For example, if the line in the story says, "They went for a walk. It was a fine day..." And you say instead, "It was a beautiful day..." The startled child may say, "Steve, it's a fine day, not a *beautiful* day." When I tell stories, I want the children to relax into the dreamlike flow of words and allow the images to wash over them. I like to avoid startling wake-up moments if possible.

I am sure you have noticed how quickly and easily a young child learns a story by heart, even without understanding the words or the plot. Memorizing comes naturally and so quickly for children, not so for most adults, including me. For me to memorize a story is a monumental effort of will. I have tried many ways to get a story into me. It definitely helps to read the story aloud to yourself while making the inner pictures rise up of what the story is depicting. Starting with the sequential flow of images and scenes in the story is a good start.

Some people write out the story by hand, pen-on-paper style. For some, writing out the story over and over works. Not for me.

The best method for me to learn a story is to memorize it bit-by-bit, a paragraph at a time. I start with the first paragraph. I speak it out loud. I try to say it again without looking at the paper. I look when I need to, until after a number of attempts with a paragraph, I can make it all the way through without looking. Then I add a second paragraph and use the paper the story is written on as needed until I can recite the first two paragraphs without looking. At some point, usually after getting the first few paragraphs down, I work on the last one or two paragraphs so I have a target to aim for, and it serve as a comforting home stretch. When I solidly have the beginning and ending, I add on to the beginning until I can go all the way through to the end.

To learn a story, I have to be alone. I like to try to tell the story in every way possible. I shout, I whisper, I sing operatic style, whatever I can think of until after a few hours I can tell the whole story. I am never really sure I have it until I tell it to others. With the first telling, I might find a gap or two in my remembering. So that night I fill in the gaps so I can tell it all the way through without glitches. All the while I picture the story unfolding before my inner eye. That helps immensely!

A method that works for some is to walk around trying to tell the story, looking at the paper as needed, and gesturing dramatically to help get the story into your body, stomping feet to accentuate. Get as dramatic as you can to help the story go in deeply. Then, when you are with the young children and about to tell the story, relax, breathe out, and let the story flow in a non-dramatic way. The dramatic antics of learning the story now can give way to the remembered story speaking directly to the children with you out of the way, as a story channeler, if you will.

If being able to tell stories by heart is important to you, you will have to find the way that works best for you. This is another case of there is no one and only way. The way that works for you is the best way for you to do it.

Chapter 10
Making Stories

Making up stories can be daunting and scary. Part of our own story might be voiced this way; "I can't create a story." "I'm no good at it." "I am not imaginative or creative enough." Do you have that critical voice?

There are some people who have the gift of making story-making less daunting and more accessible. Some have found a true calling in inspiring people to create story. One of these is Nancy Mellon, story-making-encourager extraordinaire. Nancy has written several books which are fantastic resources in this work.

To let your imagination roam free you have to tune out the voice of your intellect. In imagination anything is possible. Once you unlock the door to your imagination, trust in its guidance to help you discover the story. Trust your imagination! Don't try to complicate things by figuring it all out. Let go and allow the story to reveal itself.

One of the things our imagination can do is to make unity out of polarity, out of seeming opposites. Imagination can see form in chaos and randomness. Keep your intellect at bay, it is not your creative source.

So, how do you make up a story? How do you start?
One thing I recommend is to take out paper and pen. Once you have a starting point, let go of agenda and expectation and allow the story to come out. Take it slow it but keep writing. Don't think. Just write. You can edit later. Give free reign to your imagination, and hold back your intellect. Save your intellect for later when you are ready to edit your story.

When you write with pen on paper, you can break down mental blocks to storymaking simply because you are engaged in the physical activity of writing. Being connected to the pen opens you to imaginative expression.

As an exercise, try writing with your non-dominant hand. It is connected directly to the creative side of your brain and can connect you to your imagination. Really try it. Do stories flow out differently when you do this?

A great preparation practice for storymaking is to carry around a small pad and pen - all the time. When you get an idea jot it down. When you hear interesting things people say, jot it down. When you see the squirrels running round and round the tree, jot it down. When you are hiking and you see the bobcat, still as could be, oblivious to your presence, stalking a gopher, jot it down. When you see four small birds dive-bombing a hawk and trying to chase it away, jot it down.

Later, take a look at what you have written in your little notebook and choose one of your notes as a start for a story. And then just write.

Ignore your inner critic and commentator. It might be speaking loudly. No matter. Push on through. You surely will never be able to create stories unless you engage in the activity of storymaking.

Sometimes it is hard to find purchase with a story-starting idea. Prompts can help. A prompt can provide you with an entry point into your story. A writing prompt can be an inspiration to your imagination.

Sometimes imagination can function more freely if it is given a specific task or structure. Haiku is an example of a solid structure that allows an imagination to go wild. Prompts can give the structure from which your imagination can run wild.

Here are a few prompts, a few story-starting exercises. See if any of these speak to you. Try them all. Keep the above guidelines in mind, and remember to have fun!

1. Is there an image, a picture, whether it is a print, a painting or a photo, that somehow speaks to you? Write down the story that picture is telling you.

2. Go outside, or watch out your window. What is going on out there with the animals and plants and trees? Write about it. What are they doing? Imagine why are they doing it as part of this practice.

3. Imagine that your pet can speak. What would he tell you about? What adventures did he have?

4. Think of a traditional profession, an archetypal one like baker or fisherman. What is his or her story?

5. A character finds a special object, a treasure. Perhaps it is a ring found on a tree branch on an afternoon hike, or an unusual bottle filled with an unknown liquid in a trunk in the attic. Does he or she keep it, use it, or try to find its rightful home and owner? What happens?

6. Someone lives in a small house and there the food is almost gone. What happens?

7. Someone lives in a palace with everything they could want but no friends. What happens?

8. Someone goes for a walk, gets lost or injured, and someone comes along to help and protect him. Are the characters animals? What type?

9. You see an elderly person at the grocery store. Take a good look at him or her. What qualities do you see? Can you see hints of the life journey already taken? What

adventures has she had? What resilience has she developed? When you go home, write their story.

10. Someone takes a journey to find something. Is it to the forest? The mountains? The sea? What is the destination and what is found? And then what?

11. If you were an animal, what kind would you be? Where do you get your food? What adversaries do you have? What do you do to be safe?

12. Use the first sentence from an already written story and let it lead you down a new path in your imagination. Write the 'borrowed' first sentence on your paper, and see where it leads to. Here are a few first lines that could be fun:

A poor man had 12 children and he had to work day and night to provide them even with bread.

Once upon a time there was an old woman who had lost her husband but she was friendly with a crocodile who lived in the river nearby.

Once there was a woman who had no children. She went to her garden and found a small mouse playing by itself.

Once upon a time there lived a mother who had three sons. The mother fell ill and called her sons to her and said; "Please gather some pears from the high mountains."

Once there was a couple who were not poor since they had a portion of a rice field and a house with an earthen floor and walls of tree bark.

Once there was a fisherman who lived by the sea. He had nine daughters, all of them renowned for their beauty.

There was once, it is told, a boy who had no father, nor a mother, but an old grandmother who was very ill.

Chapter 11
More Nuts and Bolts for Creating a Story

Setting and Context

There are so many possible themes to choose from. The context for your story can be taken right out of the child's actual surroundings. The home, garden and the surrounding natural features are just the right starting point for a story for your child. There also is the wider natural world. Maybe the setting could be the forest, jungle or mountains? Human archetypal activities such as cooking, hunting, growing and building, offer a rich terrain for stories. The climate and seasons also offer possible context for a story. The animal world is loaded with possible scenarios and character panoramas.

In stories anything is possible, and anything can happen without it being questioned by the child listener. Animals and plants can speak. Magic exists. Seemingly weak characters prevail. If your imagination includes seemingly outlandish elements, let them be. It doesn't have to make perfect intellectual sense.

For the young child, everything is alive and capable of communicating with speech. It would not be surprising to a child if a plant or animal spoke in human language. Allow your imagination to include characters speaking that in your normal day-to-day life don't speak.

For the most part, I try to leave out the feelings of the characters. Instead of saying, "He's sad," I would observe, "He is crying." Rather than, "He's angry," how about, "He stomped his foot and shouted." A presentation of the facts without judgement and opinion allows the story images to penetrate to the listener's heart. As Sergeant Joe Friday said on TV's *Dragnet*, "All we want are the facts, ma'am."

Sometimes too many details can bog down the story. Practice making the story interesting while only including details in moderation.

Humor is also a wonderful addition to stories, as well as to life. Are there ways you can include some humor without getting too silly and derailing the story when you tell it?

For me, sentimentality has no place in stories for young children. Cuteness, specialness and preciousness obscure the flow of the story. "All we want are the facts, ma'am."

Structure

There is an inherent threefold structure to a story - a story has a beginning, a middle and a resolution, an ending. Each story needs a setting, a place for the story to start and characters to journey on the trajectory of the story. The setting gives us the point of departure for the story and includes characters who are involved in the events of the story.

After the setting of the scene, the story develops toward a challenge or crisis of some sort for the characters. The challenges have to be overcome as the story moves toward resolution and completion. Often someone or something wise and caring comes along to offer help in overcoming the challenges.

In stories for young children, it is important that the good prevails and the story ends with a restored sense of harmony. If there had been some sort of enchantment, the spell must be broken. If there is evil there must be redemption. If there is a problem, there must be a solution. At the story's end there is a feeling of well being and completion - all the loose ends are tied up.

To thrive, the young child needs to experience the world as good and safe so it is important to have stories where the good prevails, stories in which the difficulties are resolved and the tasks are complete. The victory of good over evil in stories confirms the child's trust in life. Make sure the story has a '**happy ending**.'

It's also important that the story feels true for the storyteller. When you have made your story, and slept on it, consider if it resonates with truth for you. It is not that the actual events are literally possible, but that the storyline has the ring of rightfulness and lawfulness for you.

A story speaks powerfully for itself. Any interpretation spoken to the children dilutes the message that the images of the story already so clearly brought. Adult minds, of course, engage in analyzing and looking for meaning in stories and everything else - practice holding back. Interpretation is an intellectual activity, and stories speak to the heart. **Don't include your interpretation of the story or state what you think is the moral of the story** to the young child.

Try to leave out the word, 'but.' For the child to surrender to the flow of a story, *'and'* is much more effective.

One resource for freeing your story creating powers is *Sing Me the Creation* by Paul Matthews. He calls it a sourcebook *for all who wish to develop the life of the imagination.*

If you need more guidance on story making, read Nancy Mellon's *Storytelling & the Art of the Imagination*. This book is chock-full of ways to get your story motor running!

Parents who did not experience storytelling in their own families as they were growing up, can discover wonderful abilities, which have been waiting perhaps for many years to come forth, hidden within them. Children, especially during their waking and going-to-sleep times can inspire our best stories. The springs of imagination well up freely through them. Sitting close to children and looking deeply into their eyes, one can often find just the right beginnings and energies for the stories they need to hear.
Nancy Mellon
(Storytelling and the Art of the Imagination)

Chapter 12
Stories for Transformation

Stories can be powerful and effective for creating behavior change in your young child. A story that portrays a challenge similar to what you and your child are experiencing with a different outcome, one you'd like to see, can be a helping story. With young children, it is an effective way to change behaviors and create new habits without much intellectualizing and explaining. A story may not make an instant change to the unwanted behavior, but it is real magic just the same. As with any approach with the young child, it takes time and repetition for change to come. For anyone, habit change takes time and repetition.

While your intellect is telling you that surely the child will know it is about him or her, actually the child will not know. The child will get lost in the images of the story and you can rewrite behaviors without him or her knowing.

I once heard Nancy Mellon explain that if we have the intention of truly helping another person, of serving his or her needs, then, when we open to that person in the realm of creative story, the picture that comes to our imagination from the other person is alive and comes from the source of healing imagination in us.

To create stories, we have to get our intellect out of the way and enter the living world of pictures, the world of imagination. And we have to learn to trust the pictures that come to us. When the storyteller part of ourselves is truly in service to the other, then healing forces can work through us and pictures arise that will be helpful to the other. Trust in the healing powers of intuition and imagination!

It helps to make a conscious, intentional connection with the intended healing story recipient by deeply thinking about the child before attempting the story creating. You can prepare for your healing storymaking session by connecting with compassion in you for that child who is challenged in some way or is challenging for you. Perhaps you are not able to truly meet his needs. Perhaps he very effectively can 'push your buttons.' He is not physically present during this practice, you are actively picturing this child in your imagination. Then you call up from inside of yourself a warm, loving wish for him not to suffer. Feel the caring feelings flow from your heart toward him. Try to feel the warmth of those feelings in your heart, and feel them as they flow from your heart toward the child. Sit in quiet and stillness for a few minutes really feeling this flowing warmth before you unleash your imagination on the helping story.

Some simple steps for making a helping story

In your imagination, transform your child's situation into one involving **animals** instead. What animal would your child be? What animal qualities do you see in your child, both the good ones and the challenging ones? Where does food come from for this animal? What other animals does this animal compete with for resources? What animals are safety threats?

Switch the gender of the central character so the child is less likely to think it is about him or her. You can include animal versions of real interactions your child has had, and you might even include some actual dialog you have heard your child speak.

In the story you make, change the names to protect the innocent, but leave the basic situation intact. If you want the characters to have names, **choose names other than those of your child and his or her friends**.

Creativity is called for in making an ending where the situation is resolved and everything comes out fine - a **happy ending**, an ending where needs are met and there is a feeling of satisfaction, an ending where the behavior of the character is just the sort of behavior you'd like to see in your child. Can you come up with a happier ending than what has been the case already, in real life?

Once you have your storyline, run through it in your imagination and see how it feels. Fix up some parts if they need it, but don't worry about perfection (whatever that is). **Keep the story simple.** If it got too complex, simplify it in the editing.

The act of trying to come up with a healing story for your child is such a powerful activity. This really is a case of the attempt being what makes the difference and it enhances your connection with the child.

When you tell your story, put your undivided attention into the story. Make the images of the story come alive in you - try to 'see' the story as you are telling it. Is there a way you can get out of the way so the story can speak through you?

Write down your story. After you have made a rough draft with pen and paper, you might want to type it up. Cutting and pasting is made easy on a computer. You will end up with a revised version that you can refer to as you try to commit it to memory. You have to somehow remember your story so you can tell it again the next day. And the next. And for a week and more. Repetition helps the story penetrate more deeply into the child's psyche, and repetition is what strengthens neural pathways. Repetition is also what forms and changes habits. Young children naturally want a story repeated over and over. Repeat the story for as long as possible.

You really can do this. Just do it! Once you have an outline of your story, a basic plot and characters, you can fix it up and fill it in. Then you can go over it again and make it more simple and make the language more beautiful. Remember you are the worst critic. Your child will be an open-minded audience, drinking in the story and reveling in the warmth and love with which the story is offered, the story that *you* made to serve his needs.

Little Squirrel in the Woods (page 71) is an example of a simple behavior changing story. It was written for a young child that tended to wander away from her adults. The adults' need for safety was triggered. A 'cure' might be this story involving a squirrel who wanders away and then experiences danger and fear, and how warmth and safety is regained.

A Short How-to List:

Make it hard for the child to recognize himself;

>Change the situation to one involving animals

>Change the gender of the central figures

>Use names other than your child's name for the characters

Make a happy ending where the main character acts in the way you wish your child would act

No moralizing or interpretation

Don't tell the child that the helping story is for him or her

Repeat the story every day for as many days as possible

Plan B - Hunting for the Right Story

Another approach to helping change behaviors with story is to use a story you heard or you read or somehow came upon that you know deep down is just the right story for this child. Still hold to these guidelines; No moralizing or interpretation. Don't tell the child why you are telling this particular story. And repeat the story every day for a while.

Perhaps you have a child who easily gives up. Maybe her medicine is the story of *The Little Engine that Could?*

Maybe you have a child who seems uncaring about animals. *The Queen Bee* could be the story that changes that. Perhaps *House in the Forest* can help him begin to say yes to animals. (Both of these are Grimm's Fairy Tales.)

Could the medicine for a child who doesn't seem to have boundaries be *The Frog King, or Faithful Henry*? (Grimm's)

Don't distill the meaning of the story for the child. Simply tell the story. The message will get through without explanation.

Healing the Body with Story

Stories can also support physical healing. That topic is a book in itself, but deserves mention here. The connection between stories and organs is gleaned by contemplating the activities of the organ and letting the images of the story move in your soul as a meditation. A story can be an imaginative rendering of how an organ functions. Four stories from the Grimm's collection are said to offer healing support for certain organs.

The King's Son who Feared Nothing gives pictures of healthy heart functioning. *Jorinda and Joringel* takes the listener (or reader) on a journey from joy, to holding your breath, and then to a climactic exhalation and return to joy. This is a lung health story.

The Frog King, or Faithful Henry offers images for kidney health. The story of *Brother and Sister* imaginatively pictures the functioning of the healthy liver.

Nancy Mellon's *Body Eloquence* is a resource book filled with story ideas to support healthy functioning of specific organs. There are sections on the major organs and stories from many cultures and traditions.

Chapter 13
A Developmental Story Sequence - What stories when?

What stories support the children in their becoming, more and more, a part of the world? Do certain stories and kinds of stories support different ages and stages of early childhood development? To some degree. Yes, and...

I caution you all from labeling a story as "appropriate" for a particular age of child, or a particular season. Lists of certain stories for certain ages are simply not helpful. Those type of lists are restrictive and eliminate possibilities. Stories are versatile and every listener can get something different from the same story. A repetitive story that might enthrall a 3 year old might be hilariously funny to a six year old. A deep fairy tale that enchants a six year old might be experienced as a melodic flow of language to a three year old without any understanding of what is going on in the story.

There is no one and only way with stories, or anything else. I offer my ideas here, and sometimes, though I try not to, my ideas sound rigid and fixed. Feel free to consider my ideas as ideas, and then, please, make your own ideas.

I would like to offer a **developmental sequence of types of story** that can support the child as she moves through her early developmental phases. Note that I have not attached ages to this story sequence.

1. Nursery Rhymes

Nursery rhymes offer seemingly nonsensical short stories. I think of these as the first stories for infants. The words are often rhyming and can be easily rendered in a melodic form. There is a built in musicality to nursery rhymes. Often the images seem silly to the adult intellect. They are easy to remember due to their shortness and rhyming words. They have a quality of rolling off of the tongue. Though they are supportive of the development of the very young child, they are fun for all ages and can be carried on all through the early years.

Nursery rhymes are nonsense. They depict the non-sense-perceptible world. They are like fairy tales in condensed form.

For instance:

Humpty Dumpty
Hey diddle diddle
Mary had a little lamb
Jack be nimble

2. Nature, garden and house stories.

These are simple stories that depict situations that could be in the young child's own life. They could be stories about the plants and animals the child might discover in her own backyard. This type of story is an imaginative narration of events in the world around us.

Some published books of this type include:

Snippy and Snappy by Wanda Gag
Peter Rabbit By Beatrice Potter
The Autumn Blanket by Susan Perrow.
  (*The Autumn Blanket* is included in *Autumn*, from the
  series of seasonal resources collected by Margret
  Meyerkort, published by Wynstones Press. In this
  seasonal series, many examples of this type of story are
  to be found.)

Tell Me a Story; Stories from the Waldorf Early Childhood Association of North America, edited by Louise deForest, has a section of these stories.

3. Cumulative stories and repetition stories.

These stories are so important for three- and four-year-olds who are experiencing significant development happening in the respiratory system. The rhythmic qualities of these repetitive and cumulative stories nourishes this rhythmic system development in the child. This type of stories also helps build up the capacity for memory.

Some published examples are:
Bringing the Rain to Kapiti Plain By Verne Aardema
The Apple Pie that Papa Baked by Lauren Thompson

And some folk stories in this vein:
Little Madam
Cat and Mouse in the Malt House
The Little Red Hen
The Giant Turnip

4. Fairy Tales

> *The fairy tale is like a good angel, given to us at birth
> to go with us from our home on our earthly path
> through life, to be our trusted comrade throughout the
> journey and to give us angelic companionship, so that
> our life itself can become a truly heart-and-soul
> enlivened fairy tale.* Ludwig Laistner (1848-1896)

I love the type of story we commonly call fairy tales. I think about them a lot. I have favorites who are like my friends and they accompany me in my life. When I am ill, I put a stack of fairy tales in easy reach for healing and comfort.

A true fairy tale is inspiration for life. Fairy tales are imaginative pictures of soul and spirit reality. One of our adult gifts is the intellect. It also is a problem because the intellect tries to tell us imagination isn't true. Imaginative pictures are a problem for the intellect. Fairy tales give symbolic representations of the struggle to become a whole and free human being. They offer spiritual truth in image form. The stories speak directly to the heart, they are received by the heart.

There is nothing of greater blessing than for a child than to nourish it with everything that brings the roots of human life together with those of cosmic life. A child is still having to work creatively, forming itself, bringing about the growth of its body, unfolding its inner tendencies; it needs the wonderful soul-nourishment it finds in fairy tale pictures, for in them the child's roots are united with the life of the world.
Rudolf Steiner (*The Poetry and Meaning of Fairy Tales*)

Fairy tales are the next stage of stories in my story developmental sequence. I think of these stories as a most important nourishment for the developing soul. They depict an individual and various aspects of the psyche, and they offer a roadmap for living life. The fairy tales answer existential questions of *who am I* and *what can I expect on this path of life.*

With fairy tales, we enter into a world teeming with depth and symbolism. You can feel there is something beneath the surface of these stories.

There is a story about Albert Einstein in which a woman *asked Dr. Einstein for his suggestions for the kind of reading the child might do in his school years to prepare him for a career of a scientist. To her surprise Dr. Einstein recommended 'fairy tales and more fairy tales.' The mother protested this frivolity and asked for a serious answer, but Dr. Einstein persisted, adding that creative imagination is the essential element in the intellectual equipment of the true scientist, and that fairy tales are the childhood stimulus of this quality!* ("Fairy Tales and More Fairy Tales" by Elizabeth Margulis, New Mexico Library Bulletin)

True fairy tales have ancient origins and come from oral tradition. They arose when humanity was more closely connected to spirit and nature. The archetypes that inform and populate fairy tales are universal.

The great archetypal stories provide a framework or model for an individual's belief system...The tales and stories handed down to us from the cultures that preceded us were the most serious, succinct expressions of the accumulated wisdom of those cultures. They were created in symbolic, metaphoric story language and then honed by centuries of tongue polishing to a crystalline perfection. Symbolic language is something that a young child seems to understand almost viscerally; metaphoric speech is the child's own speech, though it is without analytic thought...Thus even very young children can absorb the meanings and wisdom of these symbolically expressed ancient tales and use them as tools for interpreting their own day-to-day experiences. Jane Yolen (*Touch Magic: Fantasy, Faerie & Folklore in the Literature of Childhood*)

The plot, the events, are pictures of an individual's soul and spirit development. All the characters in a particular fairy tale are parts of each of us. The plot tells of individual human transformation towards a more fully actualized state of being. If this sounds like a bit of a Jungian approach, it is.

A "fairy tale," as distinct from other types of stories, is a true story in imaginative pictures of an *individual's* soul and spirit development, a symbolic representation of the struggle to become a whole and free human being. The characters in a story are all in each human being; in me and in you. The story is the story of us all. How does a spirit being descend into matter and into the sheaths of a physical human being, and find its way to connecting with all of its parts, toward self realization. The path to the marriage of one's own soul and spirit is therein articulated.

Fairy tales are true imaginative pictures, true for all time. The fairy tales give pictures of coming to terms with earthly existence in a way the young child can digest, not as intellectual and abstract explanation. When a child asks me if a story I just told is true, I want to be able to honestly say yes (or I won't tell the story).

The stories that we call 'fairy tales' offer us a description of the process of being human and the challenges of becoming more noble and just. They describe symbolically the possibilities for human transformation and show the conflicts that arise when we fail to connect with true, self-decided morality. Fairy tales can be unsettling because they show us what we still need to develop. They are a roadmap for personal human development and becoming.

Fairy tale stories are symbolic representations of the interaction of the various parts of our own psyches - we each have witches and princesses, parents, stepparents and children, kings and woodsmen, and wolves and dragons living in us. The dynamic interaction of characters in a fairy tale describes the processes of becoming human leading us toward individuation and self-actualization. That said, if a story makes you uncomfortable, don't tell it. Find another to tell. There are plenty of them!

Why do the endings often seem so harsh? Maybe we can soften them? I think it is important to leave the plot elements of a story as they are. There are deep truths hidden in the depths of the old stories. If the way a story ends doesn't suit you, find another story. There are plenty out there. Please don't change the story to suit your personal sensibilities.

G.K. Chesterton, an early 1900's British essayist and mystery writer, wrote in *The Ethics of Fairyland* about the endings of fairy tales;

> *Children being innocent prefer justice,*
> *grown-ups being sinful prefer mercy.*

I want to add an important caveat here, or perhaps a **warning label**. While 'fairy tales' are an important element of childhood, always read a story yourself first, **before** you read it to your child. You will surely find some that you are not comfortable with or that you simply do not want to read to your child. Not all 'fairy tales' are for everyone.

And even though they are symbolic of activities in our inner life, I try to find a balance in the stories I choose to tell. I want a balance between the stories where the boy is the successful one and a girl is the successful character. I want sometimes to have an elderly person resolve the story's dilemma, and sometimes a young character.

Where did it happen and when did it happen?... Anywhere, anytime..always, and for each of us.

Fairy tales give nourishment to the developing human being as seeds of moral strength. In the telling of fairy tales to children, the children receive images of strength, determination and resilience to carry through, to overcome the evil, to learn to truly see. It is not always clever and older siblings who are best suited to the task, or young, strong and handsome young men. While archetypes abound, fairy tales tell us it is possible for a human being to break out of a mold, to become something unexpected. Within is the promise that weak can become strong, poor can become rich, donkeys can become musicians, and what once was lost can be found.

A central question is, "What about the consciousness development of the young child?" The child's developing self consciousness is our primary yardstick with which to measure what stories are suitable for particular children. The years of early childhood, through kindergarten, are a time of gradual awakening from dream consciousness toward self consciousness. It is a time of gradual incarnation, first into a physical body, in a family, in a home, in a specific locality.

As the child becomes more awake, more self-conscious, and moves on to first grade, we can begin to guide her to an awareness of and knowledge about the wider world. One can say that the first stage of one's incarnation is as an individual human, then later formed by culture as a citizen of the world. As the child incarnates, we can guide her to an awareness of the world that widens as the her self-consciousness develops. In the first seven years of childhood, we are in the realm of discovering the physical body, the home and our own backyards and neighborhoods.

The deep knowledge and golden wisdom that is the fabric of true fairy tales is palpable. As one carries the fairy tale images inwardly, more of the underlying spiritual truths reveal themselves. In ancient times, initiates at the various mystery centers experienced true, direct knowledge of the spiritual world. This information was embedded in images, as stories that could speak of these truths, not to the intellect but to the heart of the listener. In long ago times the intellect was not as developed as it is today, and so for the average person to have access to that truth, it had to be woven into story. The stories spread from the mystery centers out into the diverse cultures of the earth. Troubadours, minstrels, griot and storytellers carried the stories on their travels and shared them throughout the lands as they wandered and told the tales.

Imagine a layer, a sheath, of spiritual knowledge surrounding the earth, and anyone who could access that sheath was privy to the spiritual wisdom available there. The initiate and the shaman and the wisdom bearers throughout the world shared access to this imaginal realm. When they 'received' information in this way, it was cloaked in the trappings of the culture familiar to the recipient. This is why there is archetype behind story, but the actual stories have differences in the details. Those archetypes live around the earth, and as they incarnate into culture they take on details and trappings from that surrounding culture. The true fairy tale gives information of the path an individual can take to unite the various aspects, the bodies of the human being so a balanced path in life can be attained. Fairy tales are a guide to the uniting of soul and spirit and body in the individual.

At first sight fairy tales seems to break all the rules of logic. On second sight it is clear that they have a logic of their own - not the laws of the physical world or the abstract intellect, but of the soul. In this realm of play and imagination, metamorphosis is the rule - frogs can quite lawfully change into princes. Further, though the progression of events and images does not accord with our usual ideas of cause and effect, it is nonetheless rhythmically ordered, appealing not to the brain but to the breath which understands such logic.
Paul Matthews
(Sing Me the Creation)

5. Stories for Older Children

I think there are a couple of types of stories that in general I would wait to tell until the children are a bit older, let's say, first grade and beyond. These include:

Legends - Stories about particular human beings, like Paul Bunyan and John Henry, with extraordinary capabilities.

Myths - How did it come about? How was it created?
A myth is a story that explains natural phenomena . Myths often include gods and goddesses who have special powers that can cause unusual things to occur. For instance, why doesn't the sun shine at night? What makes redwood trees so tall? Or, what are the stars?

Legends speak of the exaggerated, exploits of a "real" human being. Myth speaks to how the world and the things in it came to be, and the existence of human beings and other creatures of the earth.

When is it time for **chapter books**? Only you will know when your particular child is ready. One important capacity for readiness for chapter books is memory to be able to remember where you last left off, and the capacity to be okay with stopping where the story leaves you hanging, and waiting until next time to continue.

Chapter 14
Thoughts on Various "Fairy Tales"

If you really read the fairy-tales, you will observe that one idea runs from one end of them to the other - the idea that peace and happiness can only exist on some condition. This idea, which is the core of ethics, is the core of the nursery-tales. The whole happiness of fairyland hangs upon a thread, upon one thread. Cinderella may have a dress woven on supernatural looms and blazing with unearthly brilliance; but she must be back when the clock strikes twelve. The king may invite fairies to the christening, but he must invite all the fairies, or frightful results will follow ... A promise is broken to a cat, and the whole world goes wrong. A promise is broken to a yellow dwarf, and the whole world goes wrong. A girl may be the bride of the God of Love himself if she never tries to see him; she sees him and he vanishes away...A man and woman are put in a garden on condition that they do not eat one fruit; they eat it, and lose their joy in all the fruits of the earth.

This great idea, then, is the backbone of all folklore - the idea that all happiness hangs on one thin veto; all positive joy depends on one negative. Now it is obvious that there are many philosophical and religious ideas akin to or symbolized by this; but it is not with them that I wish to deal here. It is surely obvious that all ethics ought to be taught to this fairytale tune; that, if one does the thing forbidden, one imperils all the things provided ... This is the profound morality of fairy-tales; which so far from being lawless, go to the root of all law ... We are in this fairyland on sufferance; it is not for us to quarrel with the conditions under which we enjoy this wild vision of the world. The vetoes are indeed extraordinary, but then so are the concessions...
As in the fairy-tales, all that we say and do hangs on something we may not say and do.
But let us not forget that we have a veto.
G. K. Chesterton (*The Ethics of Fairy-Tales*)

Each story represents a wholeness. We each have the Prince and Princess, King and Queen and Dragon and more within ourselves. These stories are roadmaps for personal development, guiding us on our own path of development. Keep in mind also, as Joan Almon once said, *Fairy tales don't like to be pigeonholed.* No one likes to be labeled and defined. Fairy tales are like living beings and our relationship to them is evolving and cannot be pinned down with a particular meaning.

An adult human being of our time is blessed with a capacity for intellectual activity. Our modern tendency is for the intellect to dominate the other parts of soul and objectify all reality and experience. The intellect has become so strong we must try to overcome it and learn to think and experience with the heart. One of the magical qualities of story is that it speaks not to the intellect but to the heart so stories can be a sort of retraining for adults. I tread the path I am leading you on now with trepidation, and with recognition of the lure of the intellect. Interpretation is an activity of the intellect, yet we can try to use our hearts to discern if the intellect speaks the truth.

I think about stories, meditate about them, dream about them, and sometimes am inspired by sudden flashes of insight. I read everything I can about stories by various authors, and I read lots of stories.

Before I offer my interpretative thoughts about specific stories, I want to elucidate my perspective on the nature of the human being. My perspective is very much based on study and digestion of the work of Dr. Rudolf Steiner. I need to begin with the archetypal human being because my interpreting stories is in relation with those archetypes.

The essential core, the true individuality of the human being is spirit, which enters into earthly life clothed, as it were, in a physical body. One's spiritual individuality receives a physical body with which to reveal its gifts and unfold its destiny on earth. For the purposes of this book I often use the term 'higher self' to refer to the spirit essence of the human being. This higher self is the essential, central, spiritual core of an individual. The *higher self* experiences the world through the intermediary activity of the *soul* which receives various sense impressions and processes them, from within the *physical body*. The threefold human being is composed of body, soul and spirit.

The *physical body* has needs and instincts that reveal themselves, and it has sense experiences it wants to respond to. The *higher self* has a destiny it is trying to unfold. The *soul* lives as a dynamic interaction between the physical world of body and its surroundings, and the higher self. The soul lives in the meeting place of the higher self and the physical world. The soul of a human being is the life of desires, the realm of what one is attracted to and what one is repelled by, of sympathies and antipathies. The soul is experienced in patterns of behavior, and even patterned ways of thinking. The activities of the soul are thinking, feeling and willing. No more and no less

But we can only speak truly of the spirit if we describe how it finds expression in conditions of consciousness. We can only speak truly of the soul if we show how it lives between sympathy and antipathy, and of the body if we conceive of it in actual forms. Rudolf Steiner (*Study of Man*)

One other element of human existence still needs to be mentioned in passing - life. The physical body is the material substance that we name our body. Without some enervating force or energy, it would be simply a lifeless body, a corpse. But it does have life, and that enlivening life energy has various names from various traditions. In traditional Chinese medicine that life energy is called *Qi*. From India comes the term *Prana*. Rudolf Steiner named the life forces that give enliven and ennervate the physical the *etheric body*. This body of life energy has both maintenance qualities and formative qualities, which are especially active in young children. Thus there is a fourfold nature of the human being of physical, life-forces, soul and higher self.

You can start to see underlying organizing principles if you consider **patterns and numbers**. When numbers appear in stories, it stands for something. When there are two brothers, or three princess, or three challenges. Or three bears and three pigs. Three wishes and three guesses. Or seven dwarves, or seven ravens. Or twelve dancing princesses. And what about those thirteen wise women, one of whom didn't get invited to the party because there were only twelve plates? Through thinking and meditating I try to unravel the mysteries of stories and I often find entry through the patterns and numbers present in a story.

If there are **three** brothers or three tasks, I wonder about elements of the human being related to the number three. The threefold human being? Or the three ways humans can interact with the world - thinking, feeling and willing? Or does it have to do with past, present and future?

Is the number **four** referring to the four elements of earth, air, fire and water? Or to the fourfold nature of the human being - physical, life forces, soul and higher self? Or the Buddha's four noble truths?

Is **seven** referring to the seven special planets (Sun, Moon, Mars, Mercury, Jupiter, Venus and Saturn) that all have significant effects on our planet earth? Or to the qualities those planets evoke in the individual person?

And does **twelve** stand for the 12 constellations of the zodiac? What else can we think about that comes in twelve?

Beyond even the dream, we come to the fairy tale where many such wise fools are to be found, princes disguised as paupers, magpies who are guardians of the path.
Paul Matthews *(Sing Me the Creation)*

I'd like to offer some thoughts about a few of my favorite stories and some general thoughts about fairy tales as examples of a way of thinking. I hope that these contemplations will stimulate and inspire you to allow fairy tales to be digested in your psyche. Try to live with the questions that the stories bring up for you without being attached to finding answers.

Again, please keep in mind that these are merely my ideas - this is absolutely not *the one and only truth* about these stories. As I mentioned, intellectualizing about stories is for the grown-ups. For the children, the images speak so well on their own. For the adult, reading and rereading the same stories many times, letting them wash over you again and again, learning them well enough to tell and inwardly seeing the images as you are telling; these all will help the story to be able to speak to you on deeper and deeper levels. I invite you to let fairy tales into your heart and listen to what your heart thinks.

The Donkey

This is one of my favorites from the Grimm brothers' collection. In this tale the Queen wants to throw her donkey child into the water for the fish to eat but the King wants to nurture and raise him. The King is the nurturing, motherly aspect of this story.

The Queen wants nothing to do with the fall into physical existence from out of the spiritual world. She will not accept that the human has animal qualities and has lost his relation to his royal/spiritual origin. She wants to send it back into the etheric waters. The Donkey stands for the higher self that is clothed in an animal nature.

When the Donkey wants to learn to play the lute, he is told' "Your fingers are not made for it." You were born a Donkey, that is your karma. Remain as what you are. Be stuck in your old karma without the possibility for a future transformation.

But the Donkey has the gift of his hooves, as well as the other qualities of donkey-ness including what can be considered either as stubbornness or as perseverance. Animals are specialists, humans can be generalists with unlimited choices. Consider the human hand as an example of our unlimited options compared to the animal paw which is best suited to specific uses. The human being hidden within the Donkey wants to become something more.

The Donkey will not accept his old karma. He had a sense of his cosmic higher self and his individual, human karma. He did not want to stay a specialist! *I can grow beyond what I have been given and can develop a new capacity, a new faculty.* Humans have the possibility of creating new karma.

> *The little donkey was determined to play the lute and nothing the minstrel could say discouraged him. He worked hard and practiced regularly, and in the end he played as well as his master.*

How can we develop our new capacities and abilities out of the gifts we were born with? We do not have to be specialists like animals, but we can have ever widening skills. We do not have to rest with the old, the given, but can open new doors for ourselves to an as-yet unknown future. This is the possibility of forging our own new karma. It is hard work and requires regular practice!

As a parent or teacher, how does one help the children develop their own new faculties and abilities with which to create the future?

At some point, we all have to face ourselves. The Donkey took a walk and *came to a spring and when he looked into the mirror bright water he saw himself reflected as a donkey. He was so distressed at the sight* as are we all when we glimpse our own lower nature, our own reaction patterns. We do have the potential to develop and with strong will forces we can learn new things (to play the lute) and we can overcome our animal-like one-sided qualities and reaction patterns.

When the Prince (higher self) took off the donkey skin and revealed himself to the Princess (soul) he said, *Now you see who I am, and you also see I am not unworthy of you.* We arrive on earth, cloaked in our lower nature. We have to diligently work to reveal our higher/spiritual self.

And so we are witness to the alchemical wedding of soul and ego in which the soul and ego recognize each other and are finally joined while living in a physical existence on earth.

The Queen Bee

In this Grimm's Fairy Tale, I think of Simpleton as the part of the human being where soul and spirit meet, and his two older brothers as the feeling and intellectual parts of our souls. Simpleton, the youngest of the three princes, embodies innocence and good-heartedness, and yet also wisdom: warmth, caring and wisdom. He connects with the four elements of earthly being and is a protector and defender for them. The Ants represent the earth element, the Ducks are symbolic of water, and the Bees both air and fire. Everyone is asleep until the youngest brother, the spiritual part of the soul, accomplishes the tasks that the older soul elements could not. This youngest brother is the awakener of the human being. Three princes *and* three princesses are in this story.

Nancy Mellon explains in an article entitled *Organs Speak in Stories* that this short fairy tale, the plot and the images, *encourages us to remember the even-tempered and generous pulse at the heart's core.*

The Little House in the Forest

Also from the Grimm's collection, this is a social story. The redemption comes when the youngest of three sisters, representing our strong caring heart, cares for the animals before taking care of herself. She says "Yes" to the animals. Sometimes it is the task of the ego to say yes (different from *The Frog King* where the redemption requires a "No.").

In this story, when the transformation occurs there is a *"cracking and crashing, the door sprang open and hit the wall, the beams groaned as if they had been wrenched loose from their pinnings, the staircase seemed to be collapsing, and in the end there was a rumbling as though the whole roof was caving in."*

Sometimes change is subtle, and sometimes it comes with great noise and fanfare as in this story. And the description in the story must be familiar for anyone who has experienced a strong earthquake. This is the rocking and rolling earthquake of spiritual transformation.

The Princess in the Flaming Castle
(German folk tale from *Let Us Form a Ring: An Acorn Hill Anthology*)

This is a story about overcoming the lower levels of the self through the efforts of the higher self. In this story we see an image of awakening the unconscious will with courage and intelligence.

The Poor Man is cut off from the spiritual world and left to his own devices. The Man in the Gray Coat intervenes and brings a helping gift. The elemental forces of nature are stepping in with help.

The Bull with the golden star stands for our strong forces of will. This Bull is a spiritual being carrying wisdom from the Heavens (the heavenly meadow where he goes while the boy sleeps). Mostly we are asleep in our will, run by our habits and reaction patterns are. As we begin to wake up, our consciousness can penetrate more fully into our actions.

The Boy, a poor, young herdsman, the youngest of many children, leads a pure and innocent life. He cares for his spiritual gifts with devotion and love. He protects the beings in his care. As the youngest child, he represents a new stage of development. He shows us the possibility of connecting to our higher self, our awakened consciousness.

The King is the old wisdom, no longer true and valid. He is a placeholder - holding a place until the new impulses can take hold. He cannot keep the lower forces of greed and possessiveness from imprisoning the soul, his daughter the Princess.

The Princess is the most noble and highest aspect of the human soul. It has fallen and needs to be freed from its prison of desires of the physical world. The soul can be freed by wisdom and courageous action working as one.

There are three challenges, three initiations in the story.
The Mountain, the heights, as the head *thinking* of the earth element; the watery Sea of *feeling* life; and then the Fire and initiation of *willing* leading to the birth of the higher self. The tool for overcoming the dragon is the mighty sword of conquering truth, the sword that is *seven* 'ellen' (or meters) long, the sword that wields the power and qualities of all the seven planets.

The twelve-headed dragon of the lower self, the flames of desires, must be overcome. This is our inheritance from the constellations that we are not stuck with. We can redeem our astrology. This is an ancient heritage from an earlier stage of development. The wedding of the Boy and the Princess, of spirit and soul, is what leads us on to our next stage of development, with soul and spirit united to work together.

The Frog King, or Faithful Henry
(This is the first story in the collection from the Grimms and it is a special friend of mine!)

There are many available levels of meaning as you will see. The story of the Frog King can be considered an imaginative depiction of the physiological functioning of the kidneys. The story can be used to support kidney health, as well as to better understand the workings of the body. This is the perspective of certain holistic, anthroposophic physicians.

The story begins with a princess who loses her special plaything, a golden ball, into the water. The princess stands for the soul which can no longer receive the golden wisdom from the spirit.

The princess is weeping at the spring into which her golden ball has fallen and disappeared from sight.

There is profound grief in the soul for what is lost at birth, the access to the wellspring of wisdom and connectedness of the spiritual world, the *sleep and forgetting* that Wordsworth so wonderfully describes. The golden ball of the wisdom of the heavens falls to the earth and disappears into the depths.

A voice calls out, the princess looks around and says; "Oh it's you, you old croaker.

She recognizes the frog. The soul recognizes the higher self that it is on a path toward unity with. The frog lives in the spring. He has been enchanted. The watery realm is already an in-between place, between earth and heaven, and a frog reminds us of transformation, of metamorphosis. It was a tadpole and drastically changed to become a frog. This frog, the higher self still lives in the water, not yet fully on earth. The princess/soul is an earth dweller. The spring, and even the forest are in a border realm between sense and spirit worlds.

The king's son is a frog; the higher self is trapped in an enchanted form and not yet able to reveal its true form (as in *The Donkey*), and arise to its rightful self-leadership. Yet the frog consciousness can dive into the depths to find wisdom.

> *I believe I can help you. But what will you give me if I bring you your plaything?...I don't want your clothes, your jewels or even your golden crown. But if you will love me and let me be your dear companion, and eat from your golden plate ... and sleep in your bed.*

The frog will go into the depths and help but he has some conditions to which the princess agrees.

> *But the princess thinks, "How can he be a companion to anyone? He lives in the water with other frogs and croaks.*

The selfishness of the soul is not reigned in by integrity. So the princess gets her ball back due to the frog's efforts and she runs off. She had no intention of honoring her word.

> *"Wait, wait. Take me with you. I can't run like you." He croaked and he croaked at the top of his lungs but it did him no good. The princess ran all the way back to the palace and there was nothing left for the frog to do but to go back down into the well. The next day the frog comes knocking at the palace door, and says; "Princess, youngest princess, let me in. Don't you remember what you promised yesterday by the cool spring?*

The princess did make a promise to get her ball back. The soul made a pact to join with the spirit and now the spirit is asking the soul to remember, to once again join together.

The princess/soul knows what is at stake and is resisting her commitment. In some ways, the untransformed soul is a fun place to live, a life ruled by unbridled feelings and desires and self-serving motivation.

> The king says, "Once you have made a promise,
> you must keep it."

The wise King, the old wisdom insists she honor her word. The soul is immersed in the dilemma of saying "yes" or "no." Here she is reminded that she has already said "yes" to an agreement. But when the frog insists on getting in her bed she draws the line. Here is where the soul says 'no.' Here is the soul's boundary.

> She picked up the frog and threw him against the
> wall. But when he fell to the floor he was a frog no
> longer but a king's son with beautiful smiling eyes. He
> told her that no one but she alone could free him from
> the spring.

Only she could break the spell, only the soul can free the higher self from enchantment and the higher self can be revealed. Soul and spirit are both aspects of the self, and only we can free ourselves. As Bob Marley said, *None but ourselves can free our mind.*

They now can go back to his kingdom, as wedded soul and spirit. To get there, the young king's faithful servant, Henry, drives them in a carriage. Henry has held his heart together with three iron bands to keep it from bursting with grief and sadness. On the way to the kingdom, one by one, the iron bands crack and fall away, *because his master has been set free and is happy.* The heart (Henry) has these qualities of faith and iron strength to be able to wait until the spirit is disenchanted and free, and soul and spirit are wed. Thus the heart is freed from its self~created bondage of protection and can carry both soul and spirit to the kingdom of heaven which is all around us.

Shingebiss Redeemed

Many of you are probably familiar with the story called *Shingebiss*, with its central characters being a brave little duck, and his nemesis, the North Wind from a collection entitled *My Book House* (first published 1930). I have loved this story since my first hearing of it. The story also awakened some questions for me. I wondered how true this version was to the traditional story, and I especially wondered about those four great logs that Shingebiss had. It was to my great delight that one day in a bookstore I discovered a picture book entitled *Shingebiss: An Ojibwe Legend* retold by Nancy Van Laan (published by Houghton Mifflin Company in 1997). Upon opening the book and seeing an illustration of a green duck in its pages my relationship with Shingebiss immediately changed. Shingebiss is a green duck! He was described as a brown duck in *My Book House.* What else could have changed from the traditional tale?

The Ojibwe people, also known as Chippewa, lived in the Great Lakes region of North America. They had a close relationship with the world of nature. "Shingebiss" is a traditional Ojibwe teaching about a merganser duck, also called the *diving bird* or the *diver*, who overcomes the harshness of winter. Shingebiss is an archetypal spirit teacher, and this story has been passed down for many generations from the 'way-back time.' (Incidentally, there are many kinds and colors of merganser duck, including green, brown and multicolored.)

Though this story comes from the *oral* tradition of the Ojibwe, Shingebiss has also long been written about. Henry Longfellow included Shingebiss in *The Song of Hiawatha* (Book 2) written in 1855. And while Longfellow took liberties with traditional names and story lines, one clearly sees that this story has been around for hundreds of years. In Longfellow's version, when *Kabibonokka* (Winter Maker) heaps the snow in drifts around his lodge;

Shingebis, the diver, feared not,
Shingebis, the diver, cared not;
Four great logs had he for firewood,
One for each moon of the winter,
And for food the fishes served him.
By his blazing fire he sat there,
Warm and merry, eating, laughing. . .

Many lines from Longfellow's *The Song of Hiawatha* are echoed in Miller's version in *My Book House* .

Van Laan, in her book, mentions that she consulted an elder of the Grand Portage Chippewa Band in Michigan for her version of this traditional tale, helping to keep the story true to its ancient beginnings. Just like other true fairy tales, no human being made this story. It was received as a living teaching story and passed on person-to-person over generations.

Shingebiss is a cheerful, resourceful and brave character who perseveres in the face of a fierce and powerful foe. He has the capacity for patient waiting. He stands face to face with his own possible death and does not fear. Nor does he battle, but simply lives his life with courage and wits. In this story, Shingebiss is not helped by others; it is only through his own striving that he survives. His seeming foe is recognized as friend and fellow. The little duck is humble and without arrogance; his actions are based in recognition of the place of each individual in the world. Then they can stand as true equals. Shingebiss has princely qualities of patience and uprightness that carry him through his challenges. This little green duck is at peace with himself, and meets challenges, and meets the world, in peace.

The Van Laan story begins by explaining how Shingebiss gets his fish in summer and fall. Then we learn that Shingebiss has four great logs, *one for each of the long, cold winter months.* The duck's nemesis is named Winter Maker, and it is he who sends the cold north wind and snow to harass Shingebiss. In Ms. Van Laan's version, the traditional song in the story is translated differently from Olive Beaupre Miller's version.

The Van Laan translation;
Friend, friend,
Come in, come in
Sit with me or leave me alone.
You are still my fellow man,
Never can you do me in.

And here, the Miller translation;
North Wind, North Wind so fierce in feature
You are still my fellow creature.
Blow your worst, you can't freeze me.
I fear you not and so I'm free.

Four tests for Shingebiss are portrayed in the story, four different challenges created by Winter Maker. First there are high drifts of snow, then ice is coating the snow. Next Shingebiss is trapped by ice under the water. Finally, the icy cold Winter Maker comes into the home of Shingebiss. This final challenge is at Shingebiss' very own home fire, his hearth (heart). These tests are a spirit initiation. This story offers the example of looking at oneself without fear, and then accepting what one finds. It is only then that one is open to one's own future. Shingebiss embraces the gifts he has been given, and uses them wisely.

Shingebiss literally means *diving bird*. He is a being who goes from the airy world into the watery world of spirit, and back again. Like the frog in other stories, he is at home in both worlds. He can bring spirit wisdom to the physical world. His healing green color speaks of matter becoming spiritualized. Shingebiss is an awakened individuality who knows himself and shows us the way toward fear-free living.

Chamakanda
(The story speaks for itself on page 83)

In this humorous story from the Shona people of Zimbabwe, we meet Chamakanda, a man who is a friend to the children. He lives alone and spends his days singing and dancing and playing with children.

One of the children is curious because Chamakanda never takes off his hat. He wonders what Chamakanda is hiding. Chamakanda eventually agrees to show the boy but sternly tells him, *You must never tell anyone what is under my hat.*
The boy is a Simpleton-like character, innocent but not very mindful. Even though it is not intentional, the boy does not keep his promise so the secret of what is under Chamakanda's hat is revealed. Eventually everyone knows about Chamakanda's *big ears, big like a donkey's ears.*

Chamakanda does not want others to know that his ears are *big, big like a donkey's ears.* He cannot accept himself as he is and wants to keep aspects of himself hidden. He will not let himself be vulnerable and let others see his true self out of a fear of how they will respond.

When the community around him learns of this formerly hidden aspect through the broken promise of the boy, Chamakanda decides he must move on to a new community where he can start again without the new community having knowledge of his secret flaw, his big ears. Until Chamakanda can accept himself, his whole self, he will continue to wander the world. No community can truly accept him until he accepts himself. To evolve he must accept himself and be vulnerable. Only then will he really be an adult, able to relate to the children as well as adults.

Chamakanda is a story for all of us, and just right for this modern time!

Chapter 15
Finally, Some Stories for the Telling

Little Squirrel in the Woods
(I wrote for one particular child who liked to wander)

Once there was a little squirrel. He lived with his mommy squirrel and daddy squirrel. One day they went into the forest to gather nuts and berries for the winter ahead. His mommy and daddy said to stay near them so he wouldn't get lost in the woods. The little squirrel found an acorn. He tossed it and chased it and tossed it and chased it. He was having fun.

When at last he looked around, his mommy and daddy were nowhere in sight. He called out but there was no answer. He wandered through the forest looking for them. He met many friends in the forest. He met a chipmunk. He met two young rabbits. He met a baby raccoon. They played and played until his friends went home for their dinner. He was all alone in the forest and it started to rain. The little squirrel found a hollow of a tree where he could stay dry. He was cold and hungry and wanted to go home. The sun was setting and he was getting tired.

Just then he heard his mommy and daddy calling. He ran to them and they hugged each other. His mommy said, "We've been searching for you all over the forest." The little squirrel said, "I'm glad you found me. I was hungry and cold and didn't know the way home."

His mommy and daddy were relieved that they found him and together they went home. They ate their dinner and the little squirrel fell right to sleep, cozy and warm in his own little bed, in his own home where he belonged.

The Golden Lantern
(A story I created for a kindergarten festival)

Once upon a time there was a girl named Sophie. Her eyes were shining. Her mother and father had died and she lived alone in a house at the edge of the forest. Her sole inheritance was a golden lantern. The light of the golden lantern was always shining.

Whatever Sophie put her hand to went well. Each day she brought fresh water from the stream for cooking and washing. She tended her garden. She collected fallen branches for her fire. She always took the golden lantern with her. The creatures of the forest were her friends. They were made welcome in her house and what food she had she shared with them.

As she grew older, the light of her eyes grew dim. One evening in fall when she was in the forest and it grew dark, she noticed that her golden lantern was not shining as brightly as it had been. Over the next days, she saw that the light of the golden lantern was growing dimmer and dimmer.

One evening when Sophie was gathering wood for the fire, she met a traveler and asked him, "Who are you going through the forest with no lantern and yet the way is bright for you?"

"I am the king's youngest son. I live on the other side of the forest at the foot of the mountain of the Sun. I have come to see the girl with the golden lantern and shining eyes because they do not shine as brightly as they once did."

"Oh, but it is only my golden lantern that is growing dim," she said. "Will you help me rekindle it with a spark from the sun?"

"If that is your wish, come with me," he said.

He held out his hand and together they went through the forest. At last they came to the foot of the mountain of the Sun and began to climb. They climbed higher and higher and higher. The stars were sparkling and smiling as they made their way toward the top of the mountain. When they neared the peak and reached a small plateau, the prince said, "You must go the rest of the way by yourself. I will wait here."

So, Sophie went on. It was a steep climb and she had to crawl on her hands and knees. Finally she reached the peak of the mountain of the Sun. The first rays of dawn were at hand and reds and yellows and purples and pinks were dancing across the sky. And then the sky filled with golden light, and the warm face of Father Sun was shining over the world. Sophie called out, "Father Sun. My lantern needs kindling. Please send a spark of your light that it may brighten my way in the dark world."

Father Sun looked down and said, "My light is always shining even when you cannot see it. It is always with you. So, look at your lantern, my child. Look, it shines brightly. And as long as the light shines in your heart the light in your lantern will shine. And all will be well." Then Sophie's eyes were shining again.

"Thank you Father Sun," Sophie said, and she started down. When she came to the prince she saw his eyes were shining. Then she took his hand and they went down the mountain.

Together they returned to Sophie's house. Then the wedding was celebrated amid great rejoicing. And the golden lantern shines its warm light into their home and never grows dim.

Silver Boxes

(This is a story I wrote in response to an exercise at a Nancy Mellon workshop. The exercise was to write about parents who have fallen deeply under the spell of the computer and how the children can rescue them. Maybe this can be a healing story for adults?)

A boy and a girl lived with their mother and father in a house near a lake at the edge of the forest. They worked together cooking, cleaning, and gardening. They took care of all the things that needed doing around their house. They worked until the work was done. Then there was plenty of time for the children to play. The family ate their meals together, and mother and father told stories. The children loved the stories.

Everyday the children put out seeds and breadcrumbs for the birds. They loved to listen to the birdsong and watch the birds fly about. They especially loved the little finches who came everyday from their nests in the trees near their house.

One day, just as mother and father were finishing their busy day's work a large, beautiful snake came into their yard, and then slithered into the house. His scales were of every color, and when he moved, his scales changed colors.

Father grabbed a broom to chase the snake away but the snake spoke; "Do not be afraid of me. I am here to help"
Mother said, "How can you help?"

"I have something for you that can make your life easier. It can help in all that you have to do and you will have more time to be with your children."

Mother and Father were excited when the snake gave of them thin, silver boxes. They each picked one up and opened the lid. A pale blue light shone from inside and the parents stared.

The snake smiled and went away.

The children went outside to play. When they returned, they found their parents still staring at the boxes as if they were asleep with their eyes open. The children couldn't wake them up.

This went on for some time. The parents did less and less around the house and barely had any time for the children. The children wanted to help their parents but didn't know how. Their parents didn't listen.

"Wake up," the children said. "Wake up." The children tugged at their parents' sleeves. They parents just stared at the silver boxes. "Wake up," the children shouted and they shook their parents.

The snake heard and came back to their house. "Leave them be or I will eat you all up," he said. "We want our mother and father back. We will wake them somehow."
"Then I will eat you both," said the snake.

The children took hold of their parents' hands and dragged the parents out of the house. The silver boxes fell to the floor. The snake chased after them, and they ran and ran into the woods, the snake getting closer and closer.

The boy and girl each picked up a stick while they were running. They let the snake get even closer. At last, as the snake opened it's jaws to devour them, the boy and girl wedged their sticks into the snake's mouth so its mouth would not close and the snake could not speak. The sticks were stuck tightly and the snake couldn't dislodge them. Then snake shook its head and tried and tried but the sticks were well lodged. Then the snake slithered away into the forest and they never saw him again.

When the snake went away, the parents came to their senses again. Their eyes were awake and they smiled and hugged the children and each other. But they were in the middle of the dark forest, and none knew the way home. They were lost.

Just then seven finches flitted around the family. Two of the small birds held the silver boxes with their feet. The finches were singing and Mother and Father and the two children watched them and smiled. The finches then flew away along a narrow path. They knew they could trust the finches and they followed.

They followed the finches through the forest for a long time. Occasionally they could see a star sparkling in the sky through the canopy of tree branches.

Finally they came to the edge of the forest and the finches landed in the branches. They could see the whole night sky. It was filled with twinkling stars. They were on the shore of a lake and the lights of the stars twinkled and reflected on the water.

They watched for some time until, starting in the east, the sky lightened, and then turned rosy and golden as the first rays of dawn appeared. The finches flew over the water and the ones who were carrying the silver boxes dropped them into the lake. The boxes fell into the depths of the water, and the finches circled around the family and then flew away.

Across the lake was the house where the family lived. They could see the path around the edge of the lake that led to their house, and they began the short walk home as the new day began.

The Dragon Gate
(Adapted from the version in *Tales from a Taiwan Kitchen*)

In the heart of a deep forest, far away from any towns and villages, is a high waterfall called the Dragon's Gate.
Many carp gather at the bottom hoping to ascend the huge waterfall because those that make it to the top of the Dragon's Gate will turn into a dragon. Many carp try but few ever succeed.

Day and night the dragons guard the Gate, swishing their tails and splashing in the water to make waves, snorting out clouds to make rain and roaring thunder. Many dangers await those who attempt to climb the waterfall. Some are swept away by the swift waters, some are caught by eagle, hawk, owl and osprey, or by fishermen.

Once upon a time there was a carp who lived in a small pond hidden in a deep forest. There was always enough to eat. The little carp thought his pond was the whole world. At one end of his pond were bubbling, foaming waters that led into a rushing stream. He was afraid to get too close. As he got older his curiosity grew. He swam close to the spot and watched. He wondered what the world outside the pond was like?

One day as he was watching the foaming bubbles, his grandfather swam near to him. "What is beyond this pond," said the young carp.

Grandfather carp said; "There is a stream outside this rushing water. In this stream are many small waterfalls. If you swim upstream and climb these small waterfalls you will come to the biggest waterfall of all - it is called the Dragon's Gate. A carp who can climb to the top of the Dragon's Gate becomes a dragon. Many carp try, most fail, swept away by the rushing current, or caught by birds of prey, or foxes and bears and fishermen."

When grandfather was done speaking, he smiled warmly at the young carp and slowly swam away. When he was gone, the young carp swam straight to the foaming waters, and into the stream outside.

He swam past the many small waterfalls, avoiding the banks where hungry foxes and bears awaited. He swam in the shadows and under leaves and branches where he would not be seen by hungry birds.

At length he reached the pool at the bottom of the Dragon's Gate. He looked up at the mighty waterfall. Above him he saw hawks and other birds hunting for fish. He saw other carp try to climb the falls, only to be swept away by the rushing water and dashed upon the rocks, or get caught by the talons of the hungry birds. He was afraid but he was determined.

He leaped to the lowest ledge near the bottom of the falls, and began to make his way up from ledge to ledge, always keeping close to the rocks and rushing water, out of reach of the soaring birds. After a long time he reached the top.

A large dragon stood in the water and told him, "Go away. You are a little fish. I will not let you pass. Don't waste my time. What makes you think you can be a dragon?"
The little carp answered, "I have come this far to become a dragon. I can wait. There is plenty of time."
The dragon laughed and kept one eye on the carp. No fish would get past while he was on guard.

"I thought dragons could fly," said the little carp, "why don't you show me?"
"I can fly," said the dragon. "I can fly better than birds."
"I don't believe you," said the carp.

The dragon grew angry, and the carp dived under the water in the deep pool beneath the dragon's feet. When the carp surfaced, he said; "I don't believe you can fly. I never saw you. Maybe you are not a real dragon at all"

The dragon bellowed, "I'll show you, little fish." And the dragon leaped into the air and flapped his huge wings.

The little carp quickly darted through the now unguarded dragon's gate and waited. Soon the dragon returned. "So you can fly after all," said the carp, and he began to grow and change. The little fish was turning into a dragon. The big dragon looked at him with a smile. "I wanted you to be a dragon all the time. You are courageous and clever, so I let you pass because you are truly worthy to be a dragon." And the little carp who had now turned into a dragon, looked up at the large dragon and he smiled too. It rained that day, and when the sun came out, a double rainbow glowed over the land.

Shingebiss

(Adapted and abridged by Stephen Spitalny
from the traditional Ojibwe tale
as told by Nancy Van Laan in *Shingebiss*)

In his home on the shores of a great lake lived a little green duck named Shingebiss. During the warm months of spring and summer, Shingebiss silently paddled across the water, catching small fish as they swam near the surface.

When autumn came, Shingebiss dived down, swimming beneath the water, and found plenty to eat.

When the fierce Winter Maker swept down from the glittering land of snow, Shingebiss had four logs to keep him warm, one for each cold winter month.

No matter how Winter Maker raged, Shingebiss still waddled out across the ice. Pulling up the frozen rushes that grew by the shore, he dived down through the holes they made and got his fish for supper. Then away to home he went, dragging his fish behind him. By the balze of his bright burning fire, Shingebiss ate his supper.

Winter Maker did not like that a little duck showed no fear of him. So he sent his great north wind until deep drifts of snow covered Shingebiss' house. Inside, Shingebiss stayed close to the fire for warmth until the storm ended and he dug himself out using his webbed feet. Then he ruffled his feathers to shake off the snow and set forth to the edge of the frozen lake. Just as before, he pulled up reeds and dove in through the holes in the ice to fish. Once again he returned home with his fish trailing behind him.

Winter Maker howled and roared. He sent a storm of ice to coat the deep drifts of snow. Shingebiss stayed warm by his fire. When the storm ended, Shingebiss used his strong beak to peck through the ice. He went down to the frozen lake and again pulled up rushes and made new holes in the ice. He dove in and brought fish home for his supper. Shingebiss ate his fish and stayed warm while his third log burned.

Winter Maker was angry and sent cold, icy drafts and the chilling north wind. All the animals in their homes were shivering as they slumbered.

As soon as Shingebiss heard the winds die down, he went out just as he had before and made a hole to dive through the ice and dived in. Winter Maker blew his icy breath over the hole and the hole closed up with Shingebiss under the ice. "Ahhhhh!" cried Winter Maker. "Now I have you, little duck!"

A few moments later, near the shore where the ice was thin, there was a sound.
Pik, pik, pik.....Phit-phit-phit...
Several rushes disappeared under the ice and up popped Shingebiss with a mouthful of fish. Winter Maker was so surprised that he just watched as the little duck returned to his home with a string of fish trailing behind him.

Winter Maker made a new plan. He would show the little duck how powerful he was.
Slowly, quietly, Winter Maker crept up to Shingebiss' house. Shingebiss was just putting on his last log. Winter Maker planned to chill his house so much that Shingebiss would freeze. Shingebiss, feeling Winter Maker's chilly breath come in through the cracks in the door, knew who was there. So he sang:

Ka-neej, ka-neej,
Bee-in, bee-in,
Bon-in, bon-in,
Ok-ee, ok-ee,
Ka-weya, ka-weya!

Winter Maker knew what he was singing.

Friend, friend,
Come in, come in
Sit with me or leave me be
I fear you not and so I am free.

This enraged Winter Maker even more. So Winter Maker slipped silently under the door, and sat next to the fire, right behind little Shingebiss. And again Shingebiss sang:

Ka-neej, ka-neej,
Bee-in, bee-in,
Bon-in, bon-in,
Ok-ee, ok-ee,
Ka-weya, ka-weya!

The little lodge was growing very warm from the fire of the fourth log. And as sparks rose up, Winter Maker's icy body started to melt, and the tears ran down his face.

Winter Maker spoke; *Little duck, what kind of being are you? You act as though nothing could do you harm. Some great spirit must be helping you.*

Finally, Winter Maker flung himself out of Shingebiss' house and into a snow bank. Slowly, so slowly, Winter Maker grew colder and colder until at last, when the moon was bright and full, he into the starry sky to return to his home in the far north, and he said:

I can't freeze Shingebiss, can't starve him nor make him afraid! I will leave him in peace.

Chamakanda

(A traditional Shona story from Zimbabwe that I adapted from Ephat Mujuru's CD *Ancient Wisdom)*

Once there was a man named Chamakanda and he was a good friend of the children of his village. He liked to play with the children. He liked to dance with the children. Chamakanda was an especially good dancer.

One day, when Chamakanda had been playing with the children, he grew tired and sat down, leaned against a tree and fell sound asleep. When he woke up he reached on top of his head to make sure his hat was still there. Chamakanda never took off his hat.

A boy was sitting next to him and was watching. The boy said, "Chamakanda, what's under your hat?"

Chamakanda said, "I never tell anyone what's under my hat."

"Oh please," said the boy. "Show me what's under your hat.

"No, I never take off my hat," said Chamakanda.

The boy said, "When my father takes a bath or goes to sleep, he takes off his hat. Please show me what is under your hat."

"No," said Chamakanda, I never show anybody what's under my hat."

The boy begged and pleaded until finally Chamakanda said, "If you promise to never tell anyone what is under my hat, I will show you."

"Oh yes, I promise. I'll never tell anyone," Said the boy.

So Chamakanda took off his hat and the boy began to laugh. He said, "Chamakanda, you have big ears. Big like a donkey's ears."

Chamakanda pointed a finger at him and said, "Remember, you must never tell anyone." And he put back on his hat and Chamakanda got up and went home.

The boy also set off for his home. On the way, the boy saw one of his friends coming. He said to himself all the while, "I'll never tell anyone, I'll never tell anyone."
His friend said, "What is it you'll never tell anyone?"
"I'll never tell anyone that Chamakanda has big ears, big like a donkey's ears."

The boy continued on his way home, but now his friend knew and his friend began to tell everyone, "Chamakanda has big ears, big like a donkey's ears." Now everyone knew and they were saying and shouting and singing, "Chamakanda has big ears, big like a donkey's ears."

You could even hear the wind whispering, "Shhhh....Chamakanda has big ears, shhhh, big like a donkey's ears."

It was a long way home and the boy grew tired on the way. He sat down next to a tree in the forest, and he kept saying, "I'll never tell anyone that Chamakanda has big ears, big like a donkey's ears." When he was rested, he got up and went the rest of the way home.

In their village was a very good drummer and he decided to make a new drum. He went out into the forest to find the perfect wood for his new drum and he choose the very tree the boy rested by. He cut it and brought it home. Then he made his drum. It was a beautiful drum.

The next day was Saturday. The drummer invited all of his friends to hear his new drum. First he played his old drum.
Bum, budi, bum, budi, bum, budi, bum, bum,
Bum, budi, bum, budi, bum, budi, bum, bum

Then he played the new drum. No sooner had it touched it when it started to sing. It sang, "Chamakanda has big ears, bum, bum. Big like a donkey's ears."
Everytime he touched the new drum it sang, "Chamakanda has big ears, big like a donkey's ears."

Everybody was dancing, and singing, "Chamakanda has big ears, big like a donkey's ears."
The people of the village decided they wanted to see for themselves so they started to walk up toward the hills where Chamakanda lived. It was a long walk and on the way everyone was singing and shouting, "Chamakanda has big ears, big like a donkey's ears."

Well, Chamakanda heard them coming. He heard them coming and he said to himself, "He promised not to tell anyone."

So Chamakanda went out and hid in one of the caves near his house. When the people of the village arrived, they knocked at the door. There was no answer. So they knocked again. There was still no answer so they looked all around the house. They looked in the bushed and the trees, they looked up on the roof. They looked all around but no sign of Chamakanda.

So they went inside the house. They looked everywhere. They looked under his bed, they looked in the closets. No Chamakanda.

Now remember I told you that Chamakanda was a friend of the children? So, all the children got together and went outside. They called out to Chamakanda, "Come back Chamakanda, come back. We won't tell anyone that you have big ears, big like a donkey's ears."

Chamakanda heard them but Chamakanda did not come back. No, he did not come back. He waited until all the villagers went home. Then Chamakanda came out of the cave and went into his house. He gathered his most important things and then he set out into the wide world. Perhaps one of you might see him. You'll know him because he always keeps his hat on.

For fantasy is true, of course. It isn't factual, but it is true. Children know that. Adults know it too, and that is precisely why they are afraid of fantasy. They know that its truth challenges, even threatens, all that is false, all that is phoney, unnecessary, and trivial in the life they have let themselves be forced into living. They are afraid of dragons because they are afraid of freedom.
Ursula Le Guin
(*This Fear of Dragons*)

Chapter 16
Selections from My Bookshelf

What kind of books? Stories that make for wonders. Stories that make for laughter. Stories that stir one within with and understanding of the true nature of courage, of love, of beauty. Stories that make one tingle with high adventure, with daring, with grim determination, with the capacity of seeing danger through to the end. Stories that bring our minds to kneel in reverence; stories that show the tenderness of true mercy, the strength of loyalty, the unmawkish respect for what is good...

Cruelty, evil and greed come into clear focus against kindness, truth and honor in a well-written story. I say well-written because nothing offends a child more than having to be told when something is mean and base or noble and good. The painful spelling out of what one is supposed to learn from a story evidences the author's inability to create valid characters in a real-life plot. And it insults children.
Gladys Hunt (*Honey for a Child's Heart*)

Some of My Favorite Picture Books:

Wanda Gág wrote and illustrated many wonderful books for children from the 1920's to the 40's which include ***Millions of Cats***, and ***Snippy and Snappy.*** Both of these have that quality of repetition so important for young children's developing brains. Her black-and-white illustrations have a magical quality with so many little details for the children to get lost in. After Disney's *Snow White* movie was released, she translated and illustrated *Snow White and the Seven Dwarfs* as a reaction against the "trivialized, sterilized, and sentimentalized" Disney movie version.

The Apple Pie that Papa Baked by **Lauren Thompson**, and illustrated by Jonathan Bean, takes us through the process of making an apple pie. The illustrations are simple yet rich and in the end you can just about smell the pie. A wonderful story for the autumn.

Barbara Berger is one of my favorite author/illustrators. Some of her books I read to my daughters literally hundreds of times, and eventually I memorized *Grandfather Twilight*. Grandfather Twilight is an elderly man whose daily task is to walk through the woods as evening approaches and set the moon up in the night sky. The pictures are magical and the story is a rich yet simple poem. Two more recommendations of Barbara Berger books are *The Donkey's Dream* and *When the Sun Rose.*

Pete Seeger's storysong *Abiyoyo* was made into a book with illustrations by Michael Hays. This retelling of a South African folk tale is enlivened by the multicultural community depicted in the pictures. A wonderful story of courage accompanied by a simple song.

The Little Engine that Could by **Wally Piper** This classic first published in 1930, is the story of how a little train who has a positive attitude and determination can overcome challenges that even stronger and 'more important' trains could not, and delivers toys and food to the children on the other side of the mountain. This was a favorite of mine as a child and is imbedded in my psyche.

Eric Kimmel's *Hershel and the Hanukah Goblins* is for the older range of young children. It tells how, with cleverness and courage, Hershel overcomes the goblins and the enchantment on his town.

I like stories that describe real, archetypal work and these two are right up that alley. ***How a Shirt Grew in the Field, by Konstantin Ushinsky***, is the story of making linen from flax, in picture book form.

***Ox Cart Man* by Donald Hall**, with illustrations by Barbara Cooney, tells the story of the seasonal work activities for this 1800's New England farm family.

Mushroom in the Rain is adapted from a Russian story by **Mirra Ginsburg**. It is a fantastical story of animals getting out of the rain under an ever expanding mushroom illustrated with whimsical pictures. Like ***The Mitten* by Jan Brett**, there is almost always room for more friends to come on in and be warm and dry.

***Shingebiss; An Ojibwe Legend* by Nancy Van Laan**. I wrote about this book in depth starting on page 66. This folk tale is a wonderful story for the older young child, rich with images of challenges met and overcome. It is illustrated with beautiful woodcuts that accentuate it's wintry feel.

The Story of Ferdinand by Munro Leaf. Another classic, this 1936 story of a bull who would rather smell the roses than fight in a bull ring offers the message that fighting doesn't always solve the problem.

***The Contented Little Pussy Cat* by Frances Ruth Keller** tells about Abner who is always happy and carefree. The other animals wonder how this kitten can be so easy-going and when they find out his method they know he is on to something. Published in 1949, this beloved story from my own childhood is a profound story for adults about the path of spiritual development toward true presence in the moment.

Rosemary Wells is a must. She wrote and illustrated three **Voyage to the Bunny Planet** stories about a young bunny whose day doesn't go quite the way he wants it until he goes to the Bunny Planet where Queen Janet helps make everything okay again. Ms. Wells also offers several *McDuff* stories about a very lovable puppy. Her *Only You* is a love poem from a baby bear to his mother describing the things that only a parent can do. This is a picture book for grown-ups about connecting with young children.

Another picture book for grown-ups is *It's a Book* by **Lane Smith**. This silly book is a commentary on our digital age and worthy of reading and considering.

Stories to Foster Connectedness With the Natural World

The Lorax **by Dr. Suess**. Published in 1971, long before being "green" was a fad, the Lorax spoke for the trees and warned of the dangers of exploiting the environment. In classic Dr. Suess rhyming style, we meet the Once-ler, who comes to the valley of Truffula Trees and Brown Bar-ba-loots. The Once-ler sets about harvesting the trees and destroying the forest. Says the Lorax, "Unless someone like you cares a whole awful lot, Nothing is going to get better. It's not."

Wildflower Tea **by Ethel Pochocki** and illustrated by Roger Essley. In this lovely book, we meet an old man who lives alone. Through spring, summer and fall, he is out in nature gathering berries, blossoms and herbs. When November rolls around, he knows it is time to brew his "special tea" from all the gleanings and sit by his window to watch the snow fall.

Owl Moon **by Jane Yolen**, illustrated by John Schoenherr.
A girl and her father go out to try and see owls on a moonlit winter night. Dressed warmly, they trudge through snow. The hidden animals watch them pass. Pa makes the Great Horned Owl's call and they wait for a reply. This story tells of a nightime adventure in wintry nature of a father and daughter. It is told simply, not too many words, and it evokes the feel of a snowy night.

The Girl in the Golden Bower is another wonderful story **by Jane Yolen** and is suited for older young children. This fairy tale-like story is suited for the 6 and older crowd. Beautiful illustrations by Jane Dyer add to this wonderful story. I highly recommend this one!

Herman and Marguerite **by Jay O'Callahan** and pictures by Laura O'Callahan. I first heard this story on the car radio one day. My niece and nephew and I were spellbound. Jay

O'Callahan was telling and he quickly became one of my favorite storytellers. He turned this story into a book in which a shy earthworm and a lonely caterpillar become best friends. Through learning how to believe in themselves, and working together, they sing their dying orchard back into life.

***The Dragon and the Unicorn* by Lynne Cherry**. Ms. Cherry gives us a story of a princess who, with her friends, a dragon and a unicorn, experiences the natural interdependence in the life of the ancient forest. These friends love their forest and the peace that abides there. That peace is shattered by people cutting down trees and destroying habitat on behalf of the princess' father, the king. The pictures accompanying this story are extremely detailed, and the beautiful borders are filled with even more details.

***The Land of the Blue Flower* by Frances Hodgson Burnett**. The author of *The Secret Garden*, and many more classic chapter books also wrote a 'fairy tale' type of story suited to 6-and-ups. This longer picture book tells us that there is much to learn from the beauty of nature, from the stars and the earth. This one is a classic from 1904.

***Elsie Piddock Skips in Her Sleep* by Eleanor Farjeon,** was originally published in 1937. Elsie Piddock is a natural rope-skipper. By the time she's seven years old, she can even skip rope better than the fairies. When she is 107 years old, she returns to her hometown to try to save the children's beloved skipping grounds from a greedy, factory-building villain.

***River Song* by Steve van Zandt** with the Banana Slug String Band, illustrations by Katherine Zecca. This story is a song set to pictures. It describes the cycle of water from snow melt into streams and rivers and eventually to the sea. It is accompanied by a CD recording of the song.

Miss Rumphius **by Barbara Cooney** tells of a little girl who heeded her grandfather's advice to make the world more beautiful, and how she became the 'Lupine Lady' after traveling the world, by planting lupines wherever she went. *What will you do to make the world more beautiful?* Miss Rumphius' great-niece Alice doesn't *know yet what that can be.*

Bringing the Rain to Kapiti Plain **by Verna Aardema** describes the interconnectedness of life on the African plains, and the mutual dependence on water. This cumulative story is perfect for the little ones! It is a lovely retelling of a Kenyan folktale in simple language that hooks you right in.

Stories for Difficult Times

How do you help young children either prepare for, or deal with, death and illness in their friends and family? Death is a subject our culture tries to avoid. We just don't want to talk about it. Yet it is inevitable and simply a part of our life's cycle. Young children certainly do not need all the details of someone's illness or passing, but acknowledgment of death and illness is important in helping the child begin to embrace these aspects of life.

An effective tool for helping people of any age begin to move through grief and towards a grasp of death is story. For young children there are many wonderful stories depicting life endings and illness in imaginative ways. I think these stories can be read to children at any time, not only when there is a death in the family. That way the child is internalizing the picture or the idea of the cycle of our lives and more prepared when the inevitable occurs. When there is a loss, these stories can support the grief process. Additionally, a story might offer a vocabulary that you can use with your young child when discussing death and illness - a vocabulary that allows them to live into the pictures rather than an intellectual explanation of what is occurring.

There are tree stories that speak to this theme. *Our Tree Named Steve* **by Alan Zweibel** is the story of a beloved tree in the yard of one family that they name 'Steve.' *Yes. right there in the center of our yard, this weird looking tree grew to become the center of our outdoor life.* Steve participates in their family life over many years, gets ill and has a visit from the tree doctor and finally comes crashing down in a big storm.

Gentle Willow **by Joyce C. Mills** tells the story of a tree that develops a sickness that even the Tree Wizards cannot cure. Beautifully done in language young children can digest, this story is for anyone wanting to support children through the serious illness and dying of loved ones toward an embracing of life and love and change.

***The Fall of Freddie the Leaf* by Leo Buscaglia**. Freddie's questions and fears about dying are answered by his wise leaf friend Daniel until he eventually feels the peace of being part of nature's cycle of the seasons and of life and death.

***Thank You Grandpa* by Lynn Plourde**, illustrated by Jason Cockcroft, is the story of a girl and her grandfather who enjoy many walks in nature together over years as Grandpa and the girl each get older. He teaches her about gratitude and accepting death as it comes to the creatures of nature. And when Grandpa dies, she walks alone in the forest and knows just how to be thankful for what she and her grandfather shared. This book has beautiful images of nature. It shows the joy grandfather and granddaughter share and their acceptance that death is part of the natural cycle of life. This one is a simple story, not too wordy, that is perfect for young children.

Butterflies offer us a great opportunity for observing and experiencing transformation. Their life cycle is widely used to help develop a grasp of metamorphosis and renewal. Caterpillars are earthbound crawling things, and butterflies are beautiful flying creatures. The transformation between the two stages of life of this creature is extreme.

***Prince of Butterflies* by Bruce Coville** with amazing watercolor illustrations by John Clapp. This book seems made with slightly older young children in mind, perhaps 6-years-old and up. It tells the fictional and fantastic story of a boy who loves butterflies and grows up to be a scientist who tries to preserve their habitat. There is a wonderful scene when butterflies come en masse to the then elderly man and take him away on a flight.

A wonderful tale of aging and dying is **The Clown of God by Tomie dePaola**. It is a retelling of the legend of a Renaissance era juggler who gets old and eventually gives one last performance - his best ever - and dies knowing the gift of his last performance had made a difference.

Here are a few more picture books on the theme of death and dying:

Nana Upstairs, Nana Downstairs by Tomie dePaolo

Badger's Parting Gifts by Susan Varley

The Tenth Good Thing About Barney by Judith Viorst

The Story of Jumping Mouse by John Steptoe

A great online resource is the **Healing Story Alliance**. HSA explores and promotes the use of storytelling in healing. Their goal is to build a resource for the use of story in the healing arts and professions. On their website is a helpful article by Gail Rosen called *Seeds, Mirrors, Hands and Keys: Stories to Support Mourning.* Ms. Rosen takes us through the stages of grief accompanied by story suggestions. Read her article and remember to adapt her suggestions to the developmental level of your young children.

Some Treasured Story Collections

Each of these has some stories that I like to tell to young children. As with any collection, read the stories to yourself first to decide which ones you want to share with your child.

Folk Tales from Bali and Lombok - Margaret Muth Alibasah

Folk Tales of Uttar Pradesh - K.P. Bahadur

Gray Heroes; Elder Tales from Around the World - Jane Yolen

The Girl Who Married a Lion and other tales from Africa - Alexander McCall Smith

Grimm's Tales for Young and Old; The Complete Stories - Ralph Mannheim

Hear the Voice of the Griot - Betty Staley

The Lion on The Path and other African stories - Hugh Tracey

The Maid of the North - Ethel Johnston Phelps

Mightier Than the Sword: World Folktales for Strong Boys - Jane Yolen and Raul Colon

Not One Damsel in Distress: World Folktales for Strong Girls - Jane Yolen and Susan Guevera

Tell Me a Story; Stories from the Waldorf Early Childhood Association of North America - Louise deForest

Womenfolk and Fairy Tales - Rosemary Minard

Margret Meyerkort edited the following series of seasonal resource books, full of stories (and songs and poems):

Autumn
Winter
Spring
Summer
Spindrift
Lifeways

Bibliography

Hunt, Gladys; *Honey for a Child's Heart*

Matthews, Paul; *SIng Me the Creation*

Mellon, Nancy; *Body Eloquence*
                     Storytelling With Children
                     Storytelling & the Art of the Imagination

Meyer, Rudolf; *The Wisdom of Fairy Tales*

Quinn, Daniel; *The Story of B: An Adventure of the Mind and Spirit*

Steiner, Rudolf; *The Poetry and Meaning of Fairy Tales*

Vanamali; *Hanuman, The Devotion and Power of the Monkey God*

Yolen, Jane; *Touch Magic: Fantasy, Faerie & Folklore in the Literature of Childhood*

On the Web

chamakanda.com - my website

chamakanda.blogspot.com - my blog

healingstory.com - Nancy Mellon's website

janeyolen.com - Jane Yolen

rosemarywells.com - Rosemary Wells

bhberger.com - Barbara Berger's website